D0113985

OUR DOGS, OURSELVES

Also by
Alexandra Horowitz

Inside of a Dog:
What Dogs See, Smell, and Know

Inside of a Dog:
What Dogs See, Smell, and Know—Young Readers Edition

On Looking:
A Walker's Guide to the Art of Observation

Being a Dog:
Following the Dog into a World of Smell

OUR DOGS, OURSELVES

HOW WE LIVE WITH DOGS

YOUNG READERS EDITION

ALEXANDRA HOROWITZ

Simon & Schuster Books for Young Readers

New York   London   Toronto   Sydney   New Delhi

SIMON & SCHUSTER BOOKS FOR YOUNG READERS
An imprint of Simon & Schuster Children's Publishing Division
1230 Avenue of the Americas, New York, New York 10020
Text copyright © 2019 by Alexandra Horowitz, with illustrations by the author
Jacket photography and flap art by iStockphoto.com
This young reader's edition is adapted from *Our Dogs,
Ourselves* by Alexandra Horowitz, published by Scribner in 2019.
SIMON & SCHUSTER BOOKS FOR YOUNG READERS
is a trademark of Simon & Schuster, Inc.
For information about special discounts for bulk purchases, please contact Simon & Schuster
Special Sales at 1-866-506-1949 or business@simonandschuster.com.
The Simon & Schuster Speakers Bureau can bring authors to your live event.
For more information or to book an event, contact the Simon & Schuster Speakers Bureau
at 1-866-248-3049 or visit our website at www.simonspeakers.com.
Book design by Tom Daly
The text for this book was set in Adobe Caslon Pro.
The illustrations for this book were rendered in pen and ink.
Manufactured in the United States of America
0620 BVG
First Edition
2 4 6 8 10 9 7 5 3 1
Library of Congress Cataloging-in-Publication Data
Names: Horowitz, Alexandra, author.
Title: Our dogs, ourselves : how we live with dogs / Alexandra Horowitz. Description: Young
readers edition. | New York : Simon & Schuster Books for Young Readers, [2020] | Includes index.
| Audience: Ages 8 to 12 | Audience: Grades 4-6 | Summary: "This middle grade adaptation of
Our Dogs, Ourselves is an eye-opening, entertaining, and beautifully illustrated look about humans'
complicated and sometimes contradictory relationship with man's best friend by *New York Times*
bestselling author of *Inside of a Dog—Young Readers Edition*. We keep dogs and are kept by them.
We love dogs and (we assume) we are loved by them. Even while we see ourselves in dogs, we also
treat them in surprising ways. On the one hand, we let them into our beds, we give them meaningful
names, make them members of our family, and buy them the best food, toys, accessories, clothes, and
more. But we also shape our dogs into something they aren't meant to be. Purebreeding dogs has led
to many unhealthy pups. Many dogs have no homes, or live out their life in shelters. How is it possible
we can treat the same species in these two totally different ways? *In Our Dogs, Ourselves—Young
Readers Edition*, bestselling author of *Inside of a Dog*, Alexandra Horowitz reveals the odd, surprising,
and contradictory ways we live with dogs"—Provided by publisher.
Identifiers: LCCN 2019048056 (print) | LCCN 2019048057 (eBook) |
ISBN 9781534410121 (hardcover) | ISBN 9781534410145 (eBook) | Subjects: LCSH:
Dogs—Juvenile literature. | Human-animal relationships—Juvenile literature.
Classification: LCC SF427 .H786 2020 (print) | LCC SF427 (eBook) | DDC 636.7—dc23
LC record available at https://lccn.loc.gov/2019048056
LC eBook record available at https://lccn.loc.gov/2019048057

For all the dogs who have been,
are now,
and are yet to be

OUR DOGS, OURSELVES

CONTENTS

CHAPTER 1

BONDED

🐾 🐾 🐾 🐾 🐾 🐾 🐾 🐾 🐾 🐾 🐾 🐾 🐾 🐾 🐾

I walk down the sidewalk with my dog Finnegan and catch a reflection of us in the polished marble of the building we're passing. Finn lightly prances, perfectly in step with my long stride. We are part of the same image, connected by much more than the leash that holds us together. We are dog-human. And the magic is in that hyphen between us.

🐾 🐾 🐾 🐾 🐾 🐾 🐾 🐾 🐾 🐾 🐾 🐾 🐾 🐾

Once a dog has your heart, he has your heart forever. There's no getting away.

Scientists call this the dog-human bond. We keep dogs and we are also kept by them. We love dogs and we are loved by them. (At least we think we are. Check out Chapter Ten if you've ever wondered.)

Almost everything a dog does strengthens the connection between that dog and her person. Maybe your dog is greeting you at the front door with a wildly wagging tail. Or maybe she's chewing up your favorite stuffed animal. But she's still and always will be your dog.

Dogs have been by our side for thousands of years. Before human beings were even living in cities, we were living alongside dogs.

When early humans domesticated wolves, they began to change what wolves are. They brought wolves into their homes and took care of them because they needed animals who would help them hunt, guard their possessions, or herd the animals they depended on for milk or meat or wool. As people did this, over many years, they altered wolves for good. They didn't know it, but they were beginning to create dogs.

Today, whenever we decide to buy, adopt, or rescue a dog, it's the start of a relationship that will change us. Having a dog changes what we do in a day—a dog needs to be fed, walked, played with. Having a dog changes our minds and our hearts. It has even changed the course of our species.

Dogs in Science

The fact that dogs and humans have lived together for so many years has led to something new—scientists who research dogs. That's what I do. My job is observing and studying dogs. Not petting them; not playing with them; not looking at them fondly. Many people who want to join me in the work that we do at the Dog Cognition Lab are very disappointed to find out that we do not keep dogs here. We don't pet or even touch puppies as part of our jobs! (I'm disappointed about that too. It's always hard to keep myself from greeting and petting every new dog I meet in my lab.)

In fact, when we run experiments, any researchers in the room have to make themselves completely boring to the dogs we are studying. In our work, we try to answer questions like whether the dogs in our experiments can sniff out a small difference in two portions of food, or whether they prefer one smell to another. But as we're doing that, we can't smile admiringly at the dogs. We don't coo over them. We don't chatter with them or comment on what they do. And no sharing of adoring looks with dogs or tickling them under the chin. Sometimes we actually wear sunglasses so dogs cannot see our eyes. If a dog looks at us, we may turn our backs. In other words, we fall somewhere between acting like trees and acting inexcusably rude. (At the *end* of the study, we can finally smile at and coo at and tickle them.)

We are not trying to be unfriendly. But it's hard enough to understand what dogs are really doing without becoming *part* of what they're doing. Since one tool of animal-behavior research—eyes—is something we use all the time, it can be hard to see what's actually happening, rather than what we expect to see.

Still, humans are natural observers of animals. For most of humankind's existence, we had to be. To stay away from predators or to hunt prey, we kept a close eye on any creatures that were around. Watching animals carefully could be the difference between having dinner and being dinner.

I study dogs because I'm fascinated by them. But the things I discover about dogs tell me some things about humans, too.

Dogs and Their People

In the lab we gaze at our dogs and wonder about the ancient humans who met wolves on their way to becoming dogs. We ask what dogs feel and how dogs think, and if it's similar to human feelings and thoughts. We wonder how living with dogs has changed human beings. We try to figure out what dogs see when they look at us.

As I study dogs, I find myself seeing their owners as well. (By the way, I call us all "owners" sometimes in this book, since that's the legal term for our relationship with dogs. But I think of myself as my dogs' "person," not their owner.) The ways that people choose, name, train, raise, treat, talk to, and see our dogs deserve more attention. When we take a careful look at how we live with our dogs, we'll notice a lot of things that are odd, surprising, even disturbing—and contradictory. For instance, we sometimes treat them like animals and we sometimes treat them like human animals. We feed them bones and take them outside to pee, more like nonhuman animals. But we also dress them in raincoats and celebrate their birthdays, almost as if they were human beings. We take some breeds of dogs and trim their ears into upright triangles so that they look more like wolves or foxes—wild animals. But in making other breeds we have created animals with flattened faces to make them look more like humans.

Similarly, when it comes to the law, dogs are property, objects that can be owned, just like a chair or a backpack or this book in your hands. But at the same time, we know that dogs can do things that a chair or a backpack or a book cannot. Dogs can want, choose, demand, feel. They share our homes and often our sofas and our bed. They are family, but they are still possessions.

We love our dogs for who they are—quirky, funny, adorable individuals. We also think of dogs as members of a breed, or as having purebred parents, that should all appear and act exactly the same. But by breeding dogs to look how we want them to look—big, tiny, long-haired, flat-faced, shaggy, wrinkly, bald—we've created short-nosed dogs who cannot breathe properly, small-headed dogs who have too little room for their brains, and giant dogs who cannot bear their own weight.

Dogs have become so familiar to us that we've stopped looking at them closely. We talk to them, but we don't listen to what they're telling us. We live with them, but we don't see them for who they are.

And that's surprising, because we love dogs for being *dogs*. We invite them into our lives and our homes because we want to have an animal who lives with us, who adores us, who can be part of our lives while still being not exactly like us.

More and more people spend their daily lives away from the animals living in the world around us. We call the animals who wander into our yards or under our back porches *nuisances*. Animals in our houses that we haven't invited? *Pests*. The animals that we *have* invited inside? *Part of the family*, but also *something we own*. Dogs, part of the special category of animals that we love and live with, can connect us to the animals that surround us. They can remind us that we are animals too.

I find myself reflecting on the animals we live with and how they think about us. In this book, we'll find out more about the bond that connects us to our dogs. As we look carefully at the ways we treat, think about, and love dogs, we can learn to appreciate dogs for the animals that they are. We will also discover how some of our ideas about dogs arose.

We may even come up with new ideas about how we live with dogs today, and how we might live with dogs tomorrow.

ALEXANDRA HOROWITZ

CHAPTER 2

THE PERFECT NAME

🐾 🐾 🐾 🐾 🐾 🐾 🐾 🐾 🐾 🐾 🐾 🐾 🐾

I am sitting in the waiting room of the vet. A young doctor comes out in scrubs. His eyes are fixed on the clipboard in his hand. "Um." He pauses, puzzling at the paper in front of him, then says, "Brussels Sprout?" A young couple scoops up their miniature husky and follow the vet down the hall.

🐾 🐾 🐾 🐾 🐾 🐾 🐾 🐾 🐾 🐾 🐾 🐾 🐾

Our black dog's named Finnegan. Oh, and also Finnegan Begin-Again, Sweetie, Goofball, Puppy. I've called him Mr. Nose, Mr. Wet Nose, Mr. Sniffy-Pants, Mr. Licky. Nearly every day he gets a new name: Mouse, Snuffle, Kiddo, Cutie Pie. Plus, he's Finn.

Naming Animals

We humans are namers. If a child stares and points, an adult names what she's pointing at. Parents and toddlers pass me and Finn on the street nearly every day saying, "Doggy!"

to their kids. "Kid!" I whisper back to him once in a while.

No animal names themselves, but humans love giving names to animals. We name entire species of animals, in fact. A scientist who discovers a new species gets the right to name it, and sometimes this results in silliness.

There is a beetle named *Anelipsistus americanus*, which means "helpless American." One kind of box jellyfish is called *Tamoya ohboya*, named after the sound you might make if you got stung by one. Harry Potter fans would probably like to meet the trapdoor spider called *Aname aragog*, and cartoon watchers would be happy to spot the fungus called *Spongiforma squarepantsii*.

We don't always name animals exactly what we think we're naming them either. When one Frenchman was visiting Madagascar, he noticed the Malagasy people who live there called out, "Indri!" as they pointed to a lemur in a tree. He thought they were telling him the name of the small, furry creature. Actually, they were saying, "Look!" or "There he is!" A familiar bird is named after the Canary Islands, but the name of the islands themselves probably comes from the Latin word canaria, which means "relating to dogs."

Naming animals allows us to sort them, to figure out how they are related, to notice the differences between one kind of animal and another. It helps us to look at them carefully, to consider their lives. But sometimes it also gets in the way of seeing animals.

ALEXANDRA HOROWITZ

Scientists are good at naming species of animals, but they often frown on naming individuals they are studying. If they are observing a group of animals and need to keep track of them, scientists usually give them numbers or marks—putting a collar on a tiger, tattooing a monkey, dyeing a bird's feathers, tagging a seal, clipping certain toes off frogs or toads, or cutting a notch in the ear of a mouse.

But not naming them. When we give an animal a name, we are giving them a personality. That might change the way we see them. Should a researcher name a silverback gorilla "Giant," she might start expecting him to behave in a particular way—to be bold, strong, powerful. She might miss other behaviors—like comforting a scared youngster, or sharing his food—that don't sound like something someone with that name would do.

Jane Goodall is one scientist who did not follow the scientific custom. When she was observing chimpanzees for her famous studies, she gave them names—fabulous ones. Her chimps were called David Greybeard, Fifi, Flint, Frodo, Goliath, and Passion. She has said she just didn't know that she wasn't supposed to give them names. "I had no idea," she wrote, "that it would have been more appropriate—once I got to know him or her—to assign each of the chimpanzees a number rather than a name."

Since the 1960s, when Jane Goodall studied David Graybeard and the others, science has become more open to the idea that animals truly do have individual person-alities—the kind of personalities that we often express in names. And the truth is that scientists actually do name the animals that they study. They just don't let on. A monkey in a lab might be "Spartacus" or "Jamie's monkey" by the researchers. If he likes to bite fingers, he might end up being called "Ratfink." But when the scientist writes up the results of the experiment, they call him "the subject." Never "Ratfink."

Naming Dogs

When it comes to the dogs in my lab, however, things are different. The dogs who visit my lab for experiments are brought by their owners. And they all have names.

Do the dogs themselves know their names? It seems likely that they do. A human baby six months old can start to recognize his or her own name. These babies can't talk yet—their minds are not as developed as an adult's brain, or even a five-year-old's—and yet they know their names. So do dogs. For a dog, a name that is used over and over becomes a sound that tells a dog you are talking to her. They know.

When we publish the results of our experiments, we choose to include the dogs' names. Studies of dogs are the only kind of animal research that I know of where this usually happens. In one experiment, we asked the dogs in our study to sniff two covered plates. We wanted to see if they could tell by smelling which plate had more hot dogs. In that experiment alone, we had an almost-complete alphabet of expert hot-dog sniffers: A.J., Biffy, Charlie, Daisy, Ella, Frankie, Gus, Horatio, Jack (and Jackson), Lucy (times three), Merlot, Olive (and two Olivers and an Olivia), Pebbles, Rex, Shane, Teddy (and Theo and Theodore), Wyatt, Xero, and Zoey.

Of course all dogs have names. Giving a dog a name is one way we welcome them into the family. When a dog arrives in your home, everything changes. It doesn't matter whether the dog is a wobble-headed puppy or a fully grown adult coming wide-eyed into a new home. With a dog, things are going to be different. A new dog means you have to stop leaving plates with half-eaten sandwiches on the floor. That your favorite stuffed animal might have to stay up on a high shelf unless you want it chewed to bits.

Having a dog also means that when you walk your dog, people you see outside talk to you more. They talk to you about your dog. And one of the first things people seem to like to ask is "What's her name?"

There's lots of advice out there about naming a dog. Not a lot of science, though. Going by pet-naming trends, if you want something popular, you should probably name your dog "Max" or "Bella." Those have been among the top dog names for the last several years, at least where I'm from.

Advice flies fast and furious, and it is all over the place.

One veterinarian says that any name you give a dog should be short. Others are firm that you shouldn't give your dog a human name. Or that the name shouldn't be easy to confuse with any common command you might be planning to give a dog—you don't want a name that sounds like "Sit!" or "Come!" Some people advise a name that ends in *o* or *a*. Or definitely *y* or *e*.

If you have a purebred dog that you want to register with the American Kennel Club, he must have a name with thirty-six characters or less—spaces included. The name cannot include apostrophes or roman numerals, and it can't include the words "champ," "champion," "sire" (father), or "dam" (mother). You can't use the name of any breed for your dog—no Mr. Dachshund or Madame Whippet. If the name you want to give your dog has already been used thirty-seven times, you are out of luck and must come up with a new one.

I can only give one piece of advice I feel sure about: Name your dog something you're going to be happy saying over and over.

When you live with a dog, you wind up knowing not just the dog, but all the dog's friends. Finnegan's first best friend was Dozer, an alert dog just his size with perked ears and whiskerlike fur. His person said he had a bulldozer way about him. Finn has since been on good sniffing terms with Penny,

Ella, Hudson, Todos, and Ruby Rose. He cavorted with Moose (and liked to steal his tennis balls); he had too many play bouts to count with Bodhi, Sam, Ziggy, Bones, Jasper, and Tai-Tai. (Honestly, I'm not sure of the spelling of Tai-Tai's name; she never told me.)

Spigot, Bubbler, and Audacious

People have been giving out dog-naming advice for centuries. Xenophon, a Greek philosopher, suggested in 400 BCE that dogs should have short names that can easily be shouted. Some of the names he was fond of translate to "Spigot," "Bubbler," and "Audacious," who might have been a bold and brave dog—or maybe had an owner who wanted his dog to be bold and brave. I wish I could have met the dogs who inspired the names "Topsy-Turvy," "Much Ado," and "Gladsome."

Alexander the Great named his dog "Peritas," meaning "January." Recommended names for hunting dogs of the Middle Ages included Nosewise, Smylfeste, and Nameles. A book on hunting hounds from 1706 includes those named Bonny, Caesar, Darling, Fuddle, and Gallant.

George Washington had a Dalmatian named Madame Moose, a Newfoundland named Gunner, and spaniels Pilot, Tipsy, and Old Harry. These were the dogs he used for hunting. The house dogs were Chloe, Pompey, and

Frish. The writer Mark Twain kept dogs named I Know, You Know, and Don't Know.

In the 1800s, newspapers ran lists of names that owners had "claimed" for their own dogs. On August 19, 1876, a man named Carl claimed "the name of Rock, for my field trial setter out of J. W. Knox's Dimple, by his Belton"—in other words, his dog named Rock had a mother named Dimple and a father named Belton, both owned by J. W. Knox. That same day, other owners claimed the names Dudley, Rattler, and Beauty. A newspaper from Kentucky in 1875 lists Jack, Jip, Carlo, Fido, Major, and Rover as some of the most popular names for dogs in Louisville. There were also dogs named Bunkum, Squiz, and Duke of Kent. Children's magazines from that time have letters and stories about dogs named Bess and Blinky; Jack, Jumbo, and Joe; Towser, Spry, and Sport.

If you truly want to study the names people have given to their dogs in recent history, an interesting place to do it is at the Hartsdale Pet Cemetery, a thirty-five-minute drive from New York City. It began as a place to bury beloved dogs in 1896, and it now houses many different kinds of pets, including chickens, monkeys, and one lion.

The names engraved on thousands of stones show how dogs' names have changed in a century and a half. The earliest gravestones have no name at all, or simply mention "my pet." Before long there are dogs named Brownie and Bunty and Boogles, Rags and Rex, Punch and Pippy.

ALEXANDRA HOROWITZ

Most of the names before the 1930s were not human names. It's also hard to tell whether they refer to male or female dogs. Was Teko a boy? Was Snap a girl? No way to tell. Perhaps it didn't matter much to their owners.

After World War II ended in 1945, some dogs shared their names with humans. Sure, there are dogs named Champ, Clover, Freckles, Happy, and Spaghetti. But there also are Daniels, Samanthas, Rebeccas, Olivers, and Jacobs.

The gravestones at the Hartsdale Pet Cemetery also give a hint of how the place of dogs in the family has changed. Over time, more and more of the small tombstones give the pet buried there the owner's last name. Others refer to a dog's owners as Mom and Dad. The dogs had become family members.

At the veterinarian's office, Finnegan isn't just Finnegan. He's "Finnegan Horowitz," which always makes me giggle: what a crazy name. But it makes sense, too: He's my family, and my family shares last names.

Forty years after World War II, in 1985, a columnist for the *New York Times* asked readers to send in their dogs' names. Four hundred and ten letters arrived. Max and Belle were the most popular. Ginger, Walter, and Sam were nipping at their heels. People wrote in with dogs named after cartoon characters, favorite foods, and the colors of their coats. There were dogs named after their person's hobby (a tennis player's dog named Topspin; someone who loved their stereo system and had a barking dog named Woofer). It was common too for dog's names to have affectionate endings, like a large dog named "Binky."

Lucy, Bella, and Charlie

The first dog I got as a young adult, Pumpernickel, got her name accidentally. As soon as I met her (then named "Cujo") and her sister ("Salt-and-Pepper") in the shelter in Philadelphia, I knew I wanted to leave with her. Her sister, who was probably the one actually named Cujo, was a sweetly wild dog, racing back and forth at high speeds in the little courtyard where new owners are brought to meet the dogs. The other sister, probably the one intended to be Salt-and-Pepper (for her one white and one black front paw), sat on my feet. I chose the feet-sitter.

Then, feeling that neither name was suitable for a dog (Cujo was the name of a maniacal movie dog who attacked people! And I couldn't name my dog after the most ordinary of spices), I adopted her without a name. Shortly, though, I began talking to her—*Hi, puppy! Here you go, pup! Puppy, c'mere!* And guess what. She began responding to "Puppy" and "Pup." Oh, I was in trouble. I couldn't name my dog "Puppy"! So we browsed in the dictionary for similar-sounding words. We settled on "Pumpernickel"—she was brown-black, like the delicious bread—and called her "Pump."

Now, three decades later, has anything changed in the way people name their dogs? I decided to find out.

All I needed to do was to leave my apartment in New York City to meet loads of named dogs and their owners. At work, I e-mailed the owners of dogs who have been a part of our studies in the Dog Cognition Lab. I asked them to send in the story of How Their Dogs Got Their Names. On Twitter, I tweeted out a request for the stories of dogs and their names. A few days later, I had eight thousand names.

I loved reading the list of them all. The stories of how people named their dogs were funny, sweet, and touching. Dogs' names show that we give our dogs the very same things that they give us: love, a sense of family, and cheeriness.

What I found was that very often, a dog's name said something about the human family the dog is joining—about people that his or her owners admired, for instance. (President Jimmy Carter, writer Harper Lee, painter Mark Rothko, and actress Tina Fey: Consider yourselves the lucky recipients of the honor of having dogs named after you!) Names may say something about the sport an owner plays ("Trick" was named after a hat trick in hockey, when a player scores three goals in a single game) or the characters in books they like (Paddington from Michael Bond's *A Bear Called Paddington*, or Watson and Sherlock from Arthur Conan Doyle's Sherlock Holmes stories).

Dogs on my list were named after their personalities: Sassy, Hammy ("He was a big ham"), Pepper ("She's a spicy girl"). Coat color is still a common way to name a dog, as it has been for many years. But here is a change from the list of 1985: Many of the dogs on my list were named after people. Choosing a dog name to honor a friend or a relative is a clear way to say that the dog is a part of the family.

In my listing of nearly eight thousand names, there are in fact many nonhuman names—Fizzing Whizbee, Honey Bee, Oreo, Razzmatazz, Sprocket, Toblerone. But of the twenty most popular names on the list, nineteen are plainly human: Lucy, Bella, Charlie, Daisy, Penny, Buddy, Max, Molly, Lola, Sophie, Bailey, Luna, Maggie, Jack, Toby, Sadie, Lily, Ginger, and Jake. Today, the trend of giving human names to dogs is no longer a trend. It is just the way things are done.

Once I moved down past these twenty most popular names, I noticed how many of the names showed up only once on my list. There is one Schultz, one Sonja, one

Studmuffin. So, many dogs do have names that no other dog has. The names are as unique as the dogs who carry them. As unique as the families that chose them.

Perhaps, when a dog enters our family, we begin our relationship by handing to the dog well-plucked bits of ourselves: the books we've read, the people we've known, the feelings we have about different chocolate bars and Harry Potter characters. Maybe each member of the family will contribute a bit of the name. Dad likes Zelda the video game character; Mom likes Zelda Fitzgerald the writer: ta-da, Zelda the dog. Sometimes when children name the dog, the result is more like Sparkles, Shaggy, Sprinkles, or Doodle Butt.

The dogs themselves often become part of the naming process. "She told us her name," some people explained. Some owners called out names and waited for a response of any sort from the dog.

Before our dog Finnegan was "Finnegan," he was "Upton." We liked the name and thought it would work, but we didn't know much about our dog yet. So we tried it out for a week. We called "Upton!" after this small new slippery puppy racing through piles of fallen leaves. We cooed it at him while bending down for a face-licking greeting. It just . . . wasn't him. This dog was a Finnegan, and once we changed the name, it was clear how well it suited him.

Five years later, though, we met our Upton. Well, he was "Nicholas" at the shelter, and another name before that. He was a grown, tall, sweet-faced dog with a goofy smile and no experience with leashes. This time the name took and we had our Upton.

My own dog Finnegan comes in this category, a dog with a name that "just suited him." I like these names because they demonstrate a belief that dogs have personalities even before we meet them. When we welcome a dog into our family, we're starting out on the road to discovering who that dog really is. The first step on that road is a name.

Many people say that their dog "looked like" a Charlie, a Monty, or a Missy. Or perhaps the dog looked like another animal—bear, bunny, koala, fox, teddy bear. (Okay, a teddy bear is not actually an animal.) A bouncy dog may be named after a grasshopper. Maybe a stout dog's size warrants the name Tank.

Dog names can be silly, but some owners talk about wanting to give their dog a name with dignity. And of course there are dogs whose names combine both: goofy names with very formal titles.

I hereby present:

Macaroni Noodle the Famous Goldendoodle
Abigail Heidi Gretchen Von Droolen-Slobben
(also known as "Abby")

ALEXANDRA HOROWITZ

Mr. Tobercles, the Magnificent Muttness (also known as "Toby")

Cobber Corgwyn's Gwilym the Red Rapscallion

Grover Nipper Leaky Puccini Fuzzy Muzzle Mucho Poocho

Miller Shanner

Tchoupitoulas Napoleon

Sir Pugsley

Sir Franklin Humphrey

Sir Charles von Barkington

Baron von Doofus

Bubby von Forza

Doctor Frederick von Doom
Maximillian von Salsburg
Otto von Bisbark
Baron von Schnappsie
and
Dr. Pickles

A dog's name is not an afterthought. The specialness of your dog is matched by the specialness of his name. The name becomes almost like a set of spectacles that you put on to zoom in on the dog, noticing how much Bear is like a bear, how daring Moxie is, how much Ruth reminds you of your grandmother Ruth.

A dog gets her name, and she becomes one of us.

ALEXANDRA HOROWITZ

CHAPTER 3

PET OR PROPERTY

The first living creature I see this morning is my dog Upton. When he notices me wake up, he paws me once for a belly rub. Across the bed, Finnegan rises, shakes himself down to the tip of his tail, and comes over to greet me. Both dogs linger on the bed until I am ready to get up. They follow me down the hall, offer me toys, visit with the cat, check in on my son and his breakfast, and do their morning stretches. They will be part of our family's day.

You own your dog. You own a lot of other things too: the chair you sit on, the clothes you wear, and this book in your hands. (Unless it's a library book. Then it's owned by the library.)

With your chair, you can do whatever you want to it (more or less). You can sit on it, turn it upside down, keep it in the basement for years, or throw it out. Your chair has no say in any of this. Even if you decide to cut off its legs or draw all over it with a permanent marker, the chair must simply take it.

We think of our dogs as family, not furniture. But the truth is, legally, a lot of the things that are true of your chair are true of your dog as well.

Unlike a chair, a dog can make decisions, feel pain, and will suffer if she's abandoned. She might enjoy rolling around in leaves or snow. And she'd definitely object if you tried to draw all over her in permanent marker or sat on her. But when it comes to the rules set down by the law, the dog is treated pretty much like your chair.

There are some exceptions. It's against the law to hurt animals. But otherwise, as far as the law is concerned, you can own a dog like you own a piece of furniture.

Are Dogs Property?

When two people who are married get divorced, one or the other gets to keep the dog, and the dog doesn't get a say in the matter. If the adults can't decide for themselves who keeps the dog, a judge might step in to figure it out.

The same thing can happen to children when their parents get divorced. A judge might rule on which parent the kid might live with or split their time between two houses. If this happens, the judge will probably ask the child what he or she wants and figure out what is best for him or her. The child's opinion and well-being matter to the judge and to the law.

But a dog's? That's different. When one judge was asked to decide which half of a couple in a divorce should get dogs Willow (two years old) and Kenya (nine), he wrote that the dogs were pretty much like silverware. You don't have to think about what is best for a box of forks and knives. You don't ask whether the spatulas would be happier at which parent's. As far as this judge was concerned, the same thing was true of dogs.

But does this make sense? Is it right to say that we own our dogs in the same way we own our spoons? Dogs are part of the family, like sisters, brothers, mothers, and fathers. We might call them our companions or friends— or are they simply things?

The law says "things." My heart says no.

If I look at the dogs sharing the room with me, curled up on the pillows next to my son, the dogs are clearly more like my son than they are like the pillows. The dogs have interests, feelings, and experiences—things that pillows do not have.

Dogs are not able to tell human beings exactly what they need. Some children can't do this either (especially if they're too young to talk). But we still spend time figuring out what toddlers and babies might want—food, a clean diaper, affection. We do the same with dogs. Or at least we should.

Dogs can't take care of themselves in our society. They

don't put food in their own bowls or let themselves out for a walk. Children of all ages can't always take care of themselves either. Adults take care of children. People take care of dogs.

Dogs are *family*. And I'm not the only one who thinks so. Ninety-five percent of the people polled in the United States say that their dogs are part of their family. We play with our dogs; we share holidays, birthdays, vacations, and beds with them. We don't do any of this with our chairs, no matter how comfortable they may be.

But our laws don't treat dogs as family; to the law, dogs are property. And dog owners don't always treat dogs as we treat our beloved family members either. For instance, we leave dogs alone for long stretches of time during the day. We don't give them enough to do (so they get bored enough to search out shoes, stuffed animals, or furniture to chew). And sometimes people hurt or abandon their dogs.

How did we get to such a place, where we think of dogs as family but can still treat them like objects? How can we get our laws about dogs and the ways we treat dogs to make sense with the ways our hearts feel about dogs?

For a first step, we must go back in time.

Where Do Our Laws Come From?

In the United States, our laws about dogs and other animals are based on laws, rules, and customs that began to develop in England in the Middle Ages. Greek and

Roman laws from even further back play a part as well. Our laws about the animals we share the earth with are also influenced by a famous verse from the Bible. There, the suggestion is made that human beings "have dominion over the fish of the sea, and over the fowl of the air, and over every living thing that moveth upon the earth."

There are later verses in the Bible telling us that we need to take care of animals as well as having dominion, or rule, over them. "A righteous man regardeth the life of his beast," one reads. But the idea of dominion, of humans being in control of other animals, has had the greatest influence both on our laws and on our attitudes.

To the ancient Greeks and Romans, the world was designed for men. Men had rights, and men could own things. (When they said men, they truly meant *men*. Women—and children and slaves—were not considered full human beings with rights, including the right to own anything.) Despite the fact that much has changed since Greek and Roman times—in US law, slavery is no longer legal and all citizens have equal rights, for instance—the place of animals in our law is pretty much what it was two thousand years ago. Animals are still "things" that can be owned.

Over the years, philosophers and scientists have considered exactly how to divide human beings from other animals. The seventeenth-century French philosopher René

Descartes thought that animals were simply "automata or moving machines." Descartes was saying that he thought of animals as mechanical objects or tools, with no minds or desires or feelings of their own. If a dog whimpered or yelped, that noise didn't necessarily show that the dog was hurt or in distress, any more than a squeaky wheel or a broken horn felt pain.

More than a hundred years after Descartes, the eighteenth-century philosopher Immanuel Kant (who lived in Prussia, now part of Russia) was prepared to admit that animals were not just machines, that they had minds. But he was sure that animals could not think *rationally*, as human beings can, and they did not have what we call self-awareness—the ability to think about themselves. As far as Kant was concerned, animals do not ask questions like, "Who am I?" or "Why am I here?" This, he claimed, is what set them apart from humans.

Laws of the time reflected this kind of thinking about animals. If animals had minds or emotions at all, it was thought, they were very simple and very unlike human thoughts and feelings. And so the law didn't take into account how a dog feels, what a dog wants, or what might be good for a dog (or any other sort of animal). Laws were not concerned with whether there was a right or a wrong way to treat a dog, just as today we don't make laws about right ways or wrong ways to treat a shoe.

There was one exception to this, and that was when a

dog had done something wrong—hurt or killed another animal or a person. Dogs who did anything like this were promptly killed. This actually showed some hint that people considered dogs to be more than just mindless things—after all, a sword that had killed a person was not usually chopped to pieces or melted down.

Like the person who wielded the sword in its fatal blow, a dog owner whose dog had done wrong was held responsible and was given a fine. But it was the dog who was put to death. In a sad way, this practice showed the beginnings of an idea that a dog is different from an object like a sword, a stone, or a shoe. A dog might make a choice to do something (which a sword or a stone or a shoe could not), even if that something was violent and wrong.

In the 1800s, some of these early ideas about animals began to change. In his famous book *The Origin of Species*, the English scientist Charles Darwin introduced the idea that all living species are related. This forced people to think more carefully about the connections between human beings and animals. Jeremy Bentham, an English philosopher, pointed out that animals can clearly suffer pain, and so need to be treated humanely. During this time, we began to see laws protecting animals from cruelty.

The first such law in the United States was passed in 1821, in Maine. It made it illegal to "cruelly beat" cattle or horses. In 1829, the state of New York passed a similar law, forbidding anyone from "maliciously" killing or injuring horses, oxen, cattle, or sheep.

Notice that it was now against the law in Maine or New York to beat a cow or a horse "cruelly" or to injure a cow, ox, sheep, or horse "maliciously"—that is, hurting the animal a lot, on purpose, and for no good reason. It was still legal to beat your horse—just not cruelly. It was still legal to hurt your sheep, if you could explain that you did it for a good reason.

The animals protected by these laws were those who were worth money to humans. Cattle, sheep, and horses helped to farm the land and provided meat, milk, and wool. As they protected these animals, the laws also protected their owners from losing something valuable or that produced wealth for them. Dogs, other pets, and wild animals were not protected.

Still, having a law that cared for animals at all was a remarkable change. Decades later, in 1869, these laws were expanded to all animals, not just those who were worth money to their owners.

Laws were also passed to forbid forced animal fights so that people could watch and make bets on which would be killed—like cockfighting and dogfighting. Other laws made it a crime to neglect animals by not giving them enough food or water. The idea was beginning to take hold that animals, including dogs, had a right to a life that was free from unnecessary suffering. It was thought that animals

ALEXANDRA HOROWITZ

might still need to be controlled by humans—horses were kept in stalls, dogs were leashed. But they were supposed to be controlled with the least amount of force possible. They had a right to enough to eat and drink, and to have freedom from pain—at least from pain that had no purpose. But hitting dogs to "teach" them or whipping horses to make them run faster? The law had no problem with that.

Around this time, a new organization arose in America, the first in the country that was dedicated to protecting animals. It was called the American Society for the Prevention of Cruelty to Animals, or the ASPCA.

From its beginning, the ASPCA called for "kind and respectful" treatment for all animals. Members worked with police to shut down dogfights for public sport and to investigate claims of animal abuse and neglect. Today the ASPCA continues to rescue animals who are being badly treated, to find homes for animals who need families, and to work to pass laws to protect animals.

Changes in laws and the rise of organizations like the ASPCA went along with shifts in our ideas about animals. In the 1900s, scientists proved that animals feel pain, that they think and solve problems, and that some can even show us that they're self-aware. More and more, we began to think of animals as something more than objects. But our laws—even those that protect animals—have not yet caught up with these new ideas. Laws still treat animals as things (like chairs) that we can own.

Using Dogs

According to the law, an animal is an object (like a house or a car) that can have value. Some of them, anyway. You can see that value in the rules that govern how people can borrow money. If someone takes out a loan, that person promises to repay the money. If the borrower breaks this promise, the lender can take something away from him—a house or a car, say—and sell it, so that the lender gets their money back. This object that a lender can seize and sell is called collateral. Legally, you can use a dog as collateral, as long as that dog can be sold for money. A mixed-breed from a shelter won't work, but if a borrower owns a pricey Labradoodle, they can promise to give that dog away to be sold if they don't pay back their loan.

And, similar to objects (like chairs or shoes), dogs can be useful. They can also be used.

Millions of animals are used each year in laboratories. They are used by medical researchers, to try out new medicines or surgeries for human benefit, and by scientists trying to gain new basic knowledge. They are similarly used to test new products to see if they are safe for humans. And they are dissected in classrooms. These animals are mostly rats, mice, and birds, but a good number are dogs.

Some dogs in labs are not there to test out products or medicines. They are there to create new dogs. After a beloved family pet dies (let's hope it was after a long, good life), some owners start to think about getting another dog. That seems natural. But a few owners start to think about getting *the exact same dog* back. That's where those dogs in labs come in.

Today, for about fifty thousand dollars, owners can supply a few cells from their beloved pet to a lab. Scientists can then, using other dogs as egg donors and surrogate mothers, create a brand-new puppy that is a clone, a copy, of the pet the owner loved so much.

While the new puppy will go home with the owner, there are lots of other dogs involved who don't go home: the dog who donated eggs which will carry the pet's cells. The dog who gave birth to the puppy and nursed her. Those dogs don't get to go anywhere. They stay in the lab, like the microscopes and test tubes and the other tools that scientists need to do their jobs. Any other puppies may be born in the litter also have no home.

And once that cloned puppy gets to their new owner, will the pup actually be a copy of the first pet, down to the last twitch of a wagging tail? Of course not. Inside, the puppy's genes are the same as the first dog's. That's what being a clone means. But dogs are more than their genes. The new puppy will not grow up exactly like the first one. She will have different experiences. She will smell different smells. She will meet different dogs on the sidewalk, and she will interact with different people in different ways.

She will grow up to be a unique dog, unlike any other, just like every other dog on earth.

But laws about dogs don't always recognize that each dog is unique. They don't even recognize that a dog is more than a test tube or a specimen slide.

The law has just two categories. Something can be either a person who owns things or property to be owned. And so the law concludes that dogs must be property, since they are not persons.

Yet.

CHAPTER 4

MORE THAN ONE TYPE OF PERSON

🐾 🐾 🐾 🐾 🐾 🐾 🐾 🐾 🐾 🐾 🐾 🐾 🐾 🐾

After dinner in my house comes playtime. Finnegan likes one small squeaky ball. Upton's current favorite is a stuffed pig. Upton will joust and wrestle with anyone who stays on the red rug; Finnegan watches from the sidelines and bounds in when things are especially exciting.

🐾 🐾 🐾 🐾 🐾 🐾 🐾 🐾 🐾 🐾 🐾 🐾 🐾 🐾

Dogs offer us companionship and love. They watch our comings and goings with eager attention. What should we give them in return?

How should we treat them?

Should we treat them like a chair that we can sit on? Should we treat them like a test tube that stays in the lab when it isn't being used?

Every spring, I ask my college students this question. There is usually a long pause. They're remembering all the things we've talked about in class, all the ways that our attitudes and our laws treat animals as if they were objects. They're beginning to wonder if it's really okay to own animals at all.

After a while, someone speaks up. "Maybe we shouldn't have pets?"

Everyone groans.

They love dogs. They want to live with dogs. Quickly, they begin to brainstorm ways we could still keep dogs as pets, but do it better. We could stop breeding dogs who have little chance of a healthy life (more about this in Chapter Six). We could stop leaving dogs alone for hours and hours every day (taking them to doggie day care or hiring people to walk them during the day if no one from the family can stay home with them is a start). We could learn to read a dog's behavior so that we can understand when that dog is scared, in pain, confused, or asking us for something.

We could do this for our dogs, these animals we own.

But what if we did something more: What if we stop owning dogs? Not because we don't want to live with dogs, but because dogs aren't property that *can* be owned?

Thinking about Ownership

Some philosophers today think that we should stop living with dogs because keeping animals as pets is simply wrong. If we admit that animals, like dogs, can feel and think, that they can suffer, that they can make choices, then we cannot keep dogs trapped in our homes and yards against their will. We must respect them, and that means we could no longer own them.

The very first act of ownership that I did with my newly adopted dog Pumpernickel was to place a too-big collar around her neck. She grew into, then out of, the collar, and then I traded it for another. Her long, silky black fur grew long enough to hide it. Every once in a while I took the collar off and scratched her in the place it used to be: I imagined it felt especially good. Nowadays my dogs don't wear collars: They wear harnesses that strap lightly around their backs, chests, and bellies when we go out on leash. As common as the collar is, I love to see the long lines of my dogs' necks without the interruption of a mark of ownership.

This idea doesn't mean to say that we should toss our dogs out the door. We have invited them into our lives and must care for them in the best way we can. But this idea would also mean that we should stop breeding dogs, stop adopting new ones, and stop keeping dogs in our homes.

I can see the logic in this view, but I can't quite agree with it. I admit that I don't want to live in a world with no dogs. And I'm not sure humans can actually pull something like this off. We domesticated dogs from wolves thousands of years ago—could we figure out the best way to "un-domesticate" them, even if we wanted to?

Maybe we can agree with the idea that dogs should not be owned, but still find a way to live with them. Our first step is changing the way we think about dogs and other animals. We can't consider them objects any longer. Should we think of a dog in the same way we think of a person?

Maybe we should start by figuring out what a person is.

Defining Persons

The philosopher Plato, who lived in ancient Greece, was one of the earliest thinkers we know of who tried to define humanity. Plato said that a man (he probably was not thinking of women at all) was "an animal, biped, and featherless."

Supposedly, another Greek philosopher named Diogenes heard this definition and looked around for a two-legged, featherless animal. He took a chicken, plucked it, held it out, and announced, "Here is Plato's man!"

Plato quickly added one more item to his list of what makes a man: broad nails, rather than claws.

People have been adding items to that list ever since.

In the nineteenth century, the English author Thomas Carlyle declared that a man (again, women probably weren't in his mind) was a tool-using animal. Other animals use their paws to dig or their claws to climb or their flippers to swim. But human beings build tools: shovels to dig, ladders to climb, and ships to travel over water.

This definition worked for a time, until the scientist Jane Goodall started observing chimpanzees in the 1960s. She noticed them using grass stems to fish for termites in their mounds. The grass became tools to get the chimps a termite snack (which chimps, at least, love to eat).

Some people felt that the grass stems didn't qualify as tools, because the chimps simply picked the grass—she had not seen them change the grass stems in any way. When a person uses a wooden pole and a metal blade to create a shovel, he or she must carve the pole and shape the metal and then join them together.

However, Goodall soon noticed chimps bending twigs and stripping off their leaves to use them as tools. It truly appeared that the chimps were toolmakers as well as tool users. Later, scientists discovered lots of other tool-using animals, including ravens who bend twigs into hooks to catch grubs, and ants who use leaves as sponges to carry water.

Clearly, humans are not the only tool-using animals out there.

Over the years, we have added more items to the list of what we think makes humans different from other animals. Humans teach and imitate. We use language. We are self-aware: we know that we exist, that we think and feel, and we can think about how we think and feel. Humans have culture, which means that groups of us share behaviors and customs, like speaking a certain language, eating a certain kind of food, creating and appreciating a certain kind of art, and learning a certain cultural history.

But we keep seeing other animals do things like this. They communicate in ways that seem very much like language. They imitate each other in ways that look like teaching and learning. Some animals are self-aware enough to recognize their own image in a mirror.

It can get harder and harder to figure out what, exactly, makes human beings unique. Maybe it's time to shift our thinking to accept that there can be more than one kind of person—and that the law might have to change to recognize this. In fact, some laws have changed already.

Can Animals Be Persons?

Since 2013, an organization called Nonhuman Rights Project has tried to have the state of New York declare that a chimpanzee named Tommy is a person. Tommy is kept in a cement and steel cage outside of a trailer; if a court decides that Tommy is a person, he cannot be kept locked up like this—he'll have to be freed.

How can a chimp be a person? It's not as bizarre as it sounds. Under the law, you do not have to be a human being to be a legal person. You don't even have to have human DNA. Corporations and businesses may be considered legal persons. This doesn't mean that they brush their teeth, sleep in a bed, or eat pizza. It just means that they have certain rights that have to be respected. For example, corporations have the right to own property. They can enter into contracts. They can sue another person who has violated their rights, and they can be sued if they have violated the rights of others.

Could a chimp like Tommy have those rights too? Not yet. The court in New York decided that Tommy is not a person. But in 2016, a chimp in Argentina named Cecilia was declared a nonhuman legal person and released from a zoo to an animal sanctuary.

In 2017, the Whanganui River in New Zealand was also declared to be a person. The river is sacred to the Maori people, who consider it a living being and an ancestor. The Whanganui now has two legal guardians, one from the Whanganui tribe and one from the New Zealand government, to safeguard its new rights. Shortly after that, two rivers in India, the Ganges and the Yamuna (held sacred by Hindus), also became persons as far as the law was concerned.

Could this happen to dogs someday?

Living Property

Perhaps, one day, people will decide to think about dogs as nonhuman persons. Or we might try a different approach. We might come to think about dogs and other animals not as persons, but not exactly as things either.

A law professor named David Favre has an idea for a new category: living property—living beings that may be owned, but to whom we have responsibilities as guardians.

Considering a dog as living property would mean we think about the dog in some ways similarly to how we think about human babies. Are babies their parents' property? Do they own them? Of course not. But are they independent? Can they live by themselves, feed themselves, pick themselves up if they fall on the floor? Once again, of course not. Babies are not objects to be owned, but they can't take care of themselves either. They need someone to help them.

Or think about a woodpecker living in a national park on an impressive, huge sequoia tree. Is the woodpecker the park's—or the tree's—property? Of course not. Nonetheless, as stewards of the park, we have some responsibilities to ensure that woodpeckers' environment is intact, and that people don't hurt them. They are not persons, but they're not quite property either.

In both cases—the babies' and the woodpeckers'—we might think of them as "self-owned." They belong to *themselves*—and at the same time they can't live alone and they need care. Similarly, we might think of dogs as self-owned—and of ourselves as their guardians. That's how many people who live with dogs already think. We just need our laws to catch up with our ideas.

Legal changes like this are beginning. Two

states—Alaska and Illinois—have new laws that consider the "well-being" of a dog when deciding which person their dog should stay with when a couple gets divorced. If a judge must decide, they can think about who the dogs is most attached to, whether or not it would be stressful for the dog to move to a new house, how old the dog is, how healthy the dog is, and how the couple has shared the responsibilities for taking care of the dog, among other things.

These changes in the law show that our society is beginning to recognize something about dogs that should have been obvious all along: that they are living things, not chairs or silverware. They are alive. They have lives of their own.

Letting Dogs Be Dogs

All day long I am surrounded by dogs who are living their lives, experiencing their world, being themselves.

I start the morning with Finnegan and Upton curled up on my bed. I might spend the afternoon meeting new dogs, brought to my lab by their owners to be part of our studies. Some dogs are nervous when they get here. Some are delighted. Some are curious. Some sit quietly with their person. Some sniff and examine whatever I show them. Every one shows their personality by everything they do. When we are finished, the dogs look to their people to go home. I'll end the day sharing a meal with

my family. The people eat at the table; the dogs eat right nearby. Then we'll move to the rug or the sofa to read, watch a movie, or play. We always wind up settling down near one another—with Finnegan always wanting to be especially close.

When I think of these scenes in my home and my lab, the idea of my dogs as property that I *own* just doesn't fit. My dogs are not things; they are individuals. We are different species, but if there is any ownership here, it is shared. I am their person and they are my dogs.

What would it mean if the law considered dogs as "living property"? It would mean that we'd have to keep in mind at all times that dogs have needs of their own. When we make choices for our dogs, we would need to think about what is best for them—not just what is easiest for us.

We do not have a duty toward objects in our lives. However nice a chair may be, we don't owe it anything. But we do have a duty to our dogs. Today, our laws tell us that our duty is not to be cruel to dogs, not to make them suffer for no reason or neglect them. That's important, but not enough. To stop here is to equate *living* with the absence of neglect.

If you went through your day shut in a box, you might not be in actual pain. But you wouldn't be living a full life, either. To be fully a person, fully *you*, you need to experience all the things that humans can experience.

What do you need to be a human being? To be a kid? You need to be . . .

playing
laughing
learning
hugging
resting
dreaming
imagining
eating
loving
running

hoping
feeling
thinking
and much more.

Living, for humans and nonhumans, is not just about avoiding suffering. It is about pursuing meaning, happiness, engagements. Dogs should be allowed to experience all of the things that define their species: full dogness. Just as a bird should be flying and a kid should be playing and a pig should be snuffling in the mud, a dog should be . . .

playing
pursuing
sniffing
finding
running
resting
chasing
chewing
rolling
tumbling
mounting
nosing
touching
digging
and smelling the world all around.

Dogs should have time around dogs. They should have time around people. They should see new places, meet new dogs, try new things. They should be allowed to make choices for themselves as much as possible, allowed to decline to do some activities they might not want to. They should live as dogs, doing all of the things that dogs do.

Some of the things that dogs like to do are messy and some are embarrassing for their owners. They may pee where we don't want them to, or chew up something we care about, or hump another dog at just the wrong moment. We don't have to let our dogs do whatever they want all the time, but we do have to remember that dogs are animals. They can't always be neat and quiet and calm. They need to do the things that give dogs a full, exciting, enjoyable life. As their people, we need to make this possible for them.

In the last twenty years, scientists have learned more and more about dogs. We know that certain breeds, like shepherds, need to herd things (sheep are good, but children will do). Other breeds, like retrievers, have a drive to sprint after a moving object and chase it down. If we live with these kinds of dogs, we need to let them herd or retrieve or do what they are bred to do.

We've learned more about how much dogs needs companionship. They need to be with humans and with other dogs. In too many families, a dog is left by herself while adults are at work and the kids are at school—maybe loose, maybe in a crate. Shut away from other people, away from other dogs, limited in what they can see, smell, and touch, waiting for their people to come home.

We can do better than this.

We now know how important olfaction—smelling—is for dogs, just as vision is for humans. We've learned that they identify people and other dogs by smelling them, and that they can become less good at sniffing if we pull them away from smells. Making a dog less good at smelling takes away the very thing they need most to figure out the world around them. How can we not let them sniff, then? To let them smell the world and the sidewalk, and the tree trunk, and that dog, and you.

We've learned more about how dogs react to touch, and we understand that dogs don't like to be petted everywhere on their bodies. We know that they just put up with head pats or rough scratching—until they've had enough. We can use this knowledge to give dogs the kind of touch they like best.

In short, science has shown that all dogs have certain needs. At the same time, each dog is an individual who has ways that he or she feels.

If we think of these dogs, these individuals, as living property, then we'll have to acknowledge those needs and these feelings and that will change the ways we think of ourselves as owners. Ownership would become a privilege. We *get* to own dogs. But not if we treat them any old way. If a person shows that they can't respect a dog

ALEXANDRA HOROWITZ

as living property, that they can't provide a life that the dog deserves, the dog could be taken away and given to someone who can.

My sweet, earnest dog Finnegan sits on my soft, comfy chair, and I see him as completely different from the piece of furniture. Unlike chairs, our dogs look at us. We are seen by them. I want my actions—and the way all human beings treat dogs—to be worthy of their gaze.

CHAPTER 5

THINGS PEOPLE SAY TO THEIR DOGS

🐾 🐾 🐾 🐾 🐾 🐾 🐾 🐾 🐾 🐾 🐾 🐾

When I wake up, my first sentence of the day might be to my dogs: "Hi, fellas, how are you this morning?" I wonder about their dreams, but I don't usually ask. I ask Finnegan to creep forward for a tickle in the way he usually does—front claws gripping the sheets to pull himself along, back legs stretched out as though he's flying. I'll ask Upton if he wants a walk or if he's ready for breakfast. So a day of talking to dogs begins.

🐾 🐾 🐾 🐾 🐾 🐾 🐾 🐾 🐾 🐾 🐾 🐾

We talk to our dogs.

I've been listening for several years to what I say to my dogs, to what my family says, and to what you say. Everywhere I go I meet up with dogs—on the sidewalk, in the parks, in stores and airports, at my lab. And most of the dogs are with people. So it's not long before I hear people talking to dogs.

> **You're so cute and so smart. And worth money!**
> **I could marry you.**
> (Woman to her goldendoodle)

When I began listening, I realized that we talk to our dogs all the time. Heading down a city sidewalk in the morning, when sleepy dogs and people stumble out for their first walk of the day, I might catch two or three snippets of conversation on a single block. It's almost as if each of these people wants to show that they are not just walking along the sidewalk all alone early in the mornings. Not at all alone. They are all *with* someone—a dog.

I began writing down each overheard snippet.

> **You're going first: excellente! Awesome job!**
> (Woman to one of two small dogs—
> the one who has just peed on a post)

I couldn't make lines like this up. If I weren't writing them down right when they were spoken, scribbling them on an envelope I snatched from my bag, I probably wouldn't even remember them a minute later. I bet the woman wouldn't either. Neither she nor her dogs were paying much attention to what she said. Nobody else was listening.

I stuffed the envelope back into my bag and glanced back at her. She and her little dogs turned the corner and were gone.

From "Giddyup" to "Thanks So Much"

We've been chatting with dogs for a long time. Other animals too. A few hundred years ago, animals were all around us: Pigs walked along streets and alleys, sometimes knocking children down. Chickens were welcomed in the house. Cows were sometimes milked in the street. People talked to these animals. Probably a lot of the things they said were commands—"Coom, biddy" to a hen you want to move closer, "Bawk up" to a cow in the wrong spot.

And the animals understood at least some of what was being said to them. Working horses knew "Gee" to mean giddyup. "Heit" meant turn to the left. "So boy, there boy" was praise for a job well done.

This specific way of talking to animals reflects the idea of dominion, of human beings ruling over animals. Talk to animals was telling or commanding, not asking or wondering or carrying on conversation.

Our ideas about animals have changed over the years. And the way we talk to them has changed too. We still command animals like dogs, telling them to *sit* or *come*. (Whether the dogs actually sit or come is another question.) But we also communicate with them in another way. When we talk to our dogs (rather than giving them orders), we are in a sort of conversation. We speak *with* our dogs, not just to them.

Thanks so much. Thanks, dude.
(Man to Finnegan, who's sniffing him)

We don't talk to dogs in quite the way Doctor Dolittle does. In these books by Hugh Lofting, the doctor quits his job treating human patients when he discovers that he can speak to animals. (Plus, the animals are nicer.) When I read these books as a child, I loved to imagine talking to animals and having them talk back. The animals in Doctor Dolittle's world speak just like human beings, and the doctor chats with them as if they are friends. "Well, well!" he says to the dog, Jip, who is busy smelling out where a missing person might have gotten to. "You know that's really quite remarkable—quite . . . I wonder if you could train me to smell as well as that . . ."

In real life, our conversations with dogs don't sound quite as formal and polite as the things Doctor Dolittle says. When we talk to dogs, it's a little different.

Who's a Good Boy!

Dog owners often think of ourselves as parents and of our dogs as children. But we don't speak to dogs exactly as we do to human babies.

There is a particular way adults talk to babies—baby talk. Adults use a high-pitched, sing-songy voice that goes up and down. "Hi, baby!" they coo. They also repeat words, talk slowly, use short sentences and phrases, and leave out words like "the" or "a."

People do this with dogs, too. "Hi, puppy!" they say, in the same kind of high-pitched voice they would use for a baby. You might say, "Hey, let's go play catch," to a friend of your own age, but "Go get bally!" to your dog. It's the same kind of thing you might say to a toddler. And it turns out that we talk this way with dogs for the same reason we talk this way with babies. Dogs react to it. They respond more.

But there's one thing adults and older kids do with human babies that they do not do with dogs. When talking to a baby, an adult will often stretch out his or her vowel sounds. "Look at the dogeeeeee!" they say. This seems to be a way to help babies learn words. Since we don't expect our dogs to learn to talk, no matter how much we talk to them, we don't stretch out our vowels when we talk with dogs.

We may use the same kind of voices when talking to dogs as to human babies, but we may say things slightly differently. I say, "C'mon!" to Finnegan several times a day, but if I want my son to get moving, I'm more likely to say something a little more polite. "Come on, Sir Slowpoke," "Will you come with me, kiddo?," or "Let's get going, please," are things I might say to him. I lift up my eyebrows and use a high voice to say, "What's this?" to my dogs, but not to my kid. And I don't tell my son, "Go to your bed!" or "Sit!"

I did catch myself saying "Good boy!" once to my son when he was very little. Never again.

Things We Say to Our Dogs

What are you even doing? I don't understand you.
(Woman to her very sniffy black-and-white dog)

I do talk to my dogs, though, quite a bit. Of course, I don't expect them to answer back. If I thought they might, it would change what I'd say. The Yurok Indians of California valued their hunting dogs greatly, but they did not talk to them or even name them. If they did, they believed, the dogs might one day answer—and then the natural order of the world would be overturned. Catastrophe might follow.

This isn't something that I generally worry about, and I'm glad. If there is a dog around (and if I'm not running a study with that dog in my lab), I like to talk to him.

I don't know, you'll have to ask him. They're his.
(Nonchalant dog's owner to another dog sniffing at his pocket)

After scribbling down several hundred of comments that I heard owners say to dogs, I began to notice a pattern. The woman who praised her sweater-wearing dog for peeing fits into a very common category: the Mom

Commentator. With her eyes fixed on her dog, she notices everything he does. And she's gotta talk about it:

You've got a lot to learn! A lot to learn! (Woman to her dachshund puppy on the sidewalk)

What's with all the grass this morning, dog? (Woman to dew-licking, long-haired mutt)

Did you make a friend? (Woman to her approaching, wagging dog)

I know you got excited when you saw another puppy . . . but I need my arm to remain in the socket. (Woman to leash-tugging retriever)

You can sit all you want when we're home. (Woman to dog not going anywhere)

You are B-A-D. (Woman to keen-spelling dog)

Most of the Mom Commentators I recorded were women. Actually, research shows that women talk to their dogs about six times more often than men do. When talking to their dogs, women also speak more often, more quickly, and longer than men do.

That's not to say that men don't participate in Mom Commentary at all. They definitely do:

Be nice! When you get tired, you get nasty. (Man to rambunctiously playing dog)

Oh come on, now, give me a break. It's just me. (Man to barking dog)

Buddy, you can't stop in the middle of the street. (Man to loitering dog)

Okay, I got it, kiddo. I can definitely hear that. It's coming any minute now. Almost there. It's very exciting. (Man to dog howling for a treat)

One thing that both men and women often talk about to their dogs is how hard it is for them to understand what their dog is doing. I call this the Confused Human:

Come on! It's a lamppost. (Man to dog enjoying the finer pleasures of sniffing a lamppost on a rainy evening)

Two-dog butt-sniff! Wow! (Woman to yellow Lab being well investigated)

I just don't see what's so interesting. (Woman to nose-on-the-ground Pekingese)

Another common category of dog talker is the Cheering

Squad, encouraging and celebrating the things that their dogs do:

Good stop. I really liked that halt, guys. (Dog walker to the five dogs she has on leash)

At least down the block, baby. (Woman to her large, unmoving bulldog)

C'mon, you made it the whole way. One more step! (Man on top step to puppy sprawled on second-to-last step)

Let's lead! Leader! YAY! (Woman leaving house with tiny dog)

Go on, get a good sniff of his wisdom. (Woman to dog nosing another dog's graying muzzle)

Dog owners also spend a lot of time on a third category: Instructions. Of course this includes the usual commands—sit, stay, come, and roll over. (Why on earth does a dog need to roll over?) But people also tell their dogs to do other things—even when some of those things are very unlikely or perhaps impossible:

Okay you guys: share. (Man to two dogs being given a plate to lick clean)

No pizza! No! (Woman to a Yorkshire terrier eyeing a fallen slice on the sidewalk)

No coyote scat before breakfast, dogs. (Woman to dogs who could work as poop-detection dogs)

If you make it to the end of the fence, you get a

biscuit. If you lie down, no biscuit. (Woman to corgi who's probably not going to make it to the end of the fence)

Not now. We'll smell that on the way back. (Woman to dog very interested in a particular patch of sidewalk)

Go run! Go play! Wait, not in the mud! (Woman to a Labrador who's now in the mud)

Go get the ball! Get the ball! Get the . . . Okay. I'll get it. (Woman to non-retrieving retriever)

C'mon, Sir Drags-A-Lot. (Woman to hot dog, in hot park, in hot city)

A little privacy, man. (Woman to dog eagerly sniffing pooing dog)

Be part of the solution, buddy. (Woman to misbehaving dog)

I see you doing weird stuff. Cut it out. (Woman to one of her four small dogs)

Leave it. We have better ones at home. (Man to dog desperately searching for lost tennis ball)

Gimme paw! Gimme paw! (Elderly man on the street to three-legged dog)

Often these instructions (like the man encouraging the three-legged dog to hand him a paw) are repeated over and over, in a way that we would never do in ordinary conversation:

Go go go go go, let's go, let's go. (Woman to dog nosing curb)

STOP. STOP IT. STOP. STOP. STOP! (Woman with ball to Labrador barking for ball)

Kill it! Kill it! Kill it! Kill it. Kill it, yay! (Woman to dog with a soft toy)

We don't just tell our dogs to do things—we ask them things as well. We may even wait as if for a reply, but we know that no answer is coming. These snippets make up the Forever Unanswered Questions category:

Am I still interesting? (Woman to puppy, interested in something else)

What, are you reinventing the poo? (Woman to long-pooing dog)

Did you get a new toy? Did you get a new toy? DID YOU GET A NEW TOY? (Woman to dog waiting with toy in his mouth)

What's your name, baby? (Woman to "Spike")

Are you coming to the park? Or am I going alone? (Man to long-eared, sad-eyed dog)

Would you guys like to be in a book group? (Woman to dogs in dog park)

Why do you always do that when she's sniffing? (Man with two dogs, one pulling eastward, one nose downward)

Hi, honey. Did you vote? (Woman to

pleased-looking dog outside voting center)

And finally, there's the category I call "We've Discussed This," when owners tell dogs things they both already know (in theory):

We both know we have to go now. (Woman to dog playing happily in snow)
Seriously? (Woman to long-peeing dog)
We've talked about this: No eating stuff you find on the street. (Man to dog foraging for food)
You remember, how we were going to cooperate? Good girl. (Woman to unresponsive dog)
Hey! Stop it! [whispered] We talked about this yesterday. (Woman to lunging dog)

Things Kids Say to Their Dogs

One interesting question that research hasn't settled yet is this: Do kids talk to their dogs in the same way that adults do? At the moment, I'm not sure.

I've done a small amount of research on this question. Some things that kids say to dogs do seem to fall into the same categories as the things that adults say.

Cheering Squad:
Hey dog, you're a check-plus dog! (Boy to very good dachshund)

Forever Unanswered Questions:
Good heavens, where have you sprung from?!? (Boy

to two dogs who suddenly appeared around the corner)

Is that because you only respond the second time? (Boy to a dog named Echo)

Instructions:

Okay, let's run up the street! (Girl to new puppy on leash, not going anywhere)

Eat this. Eat this. Eat it. Eat it. Eat it. Eat it! (Girl playing with dog)

Do it. Do it. Do it. Do it. Go get it! (Girl to dog with toy)

It could be that kids mostly talk to dogs in a way that is actually quite different from adults. We need more research to be sure. Maybe you can provide it. Stuff a notebook or a sheet of paper in your backpack or your pocket and head out onto the sidewalks. If you catch a kid talking to a dog, pause and write down what they are saying. Or listen to yourself talking to the dogs you encounter. Compare it to the ways adults talk to dogs and see what you discover.

🐾 🐾 🐾

One thing that we do know is that we talk to dogs differently when there are other people around. In this case, the dogs serve as a connection between people. They become a way for people to talk to each other. When we ask dogs "What's your name?", the dogs never answer. But their owners might.

If I'm by myself, I might feel a little uncertain about a person I don't know approaching me on the street. But Finnegan greets everyone with a smile and a wag. Both the other person and I can connect with each other by talking to Finnegan. "Hi, you! What a great day for a walk!" someone might say to Finn when we're out. "You're so shiny!" people tell him. "Thanks! I polish him every day, don't I, Finn?" I often answer.

At a dog park, a new dog is greeted by the noses of the dogs who are regulars—and by the attention of their owners. "Who are you?" "What a sweetie you are." "Oh, you're a jumper!" After talking to the dog and looking at the dog, the people can raise their eyes to the dog's owner. When the humans are done chatting, the conversation will usually be ended by returning the talk to the dog. "Bye-bye, Max." "See you tomorrow, little guy."

Dogs do an excellent job of bringing people together. A dog can be your friend, and she can also be the link that connects you to other friends, human ones.

People Talking for Their Dogs

Humans talk and talk, but our dogs are silent. Some scientists think we actually like it this way—dogs are all listening and no talking back. It's the perfect conversation. Or perhaps the quietness of dogs is just something of a relief after all the talking we listen hear all day at home, at school, and with our friends.

But soon enough, we fill in the dog's side of the script: we start providing words for them. In England during the 1800s, people wrote autobiographies for their dogs, telling of the puppy's youth, upbringing, adventures, and the wisdom of old age. Some of these dogs, apparently, even "wrote" notes to their own doctors. "I feel 'real sick' this morning," one explained. "You must promise not to tell mother, but she gave a dinner last evening, and I *did* enjoy myself . . . Do you think it is possible for [that] to have made me feel as I do? . . . Your grateful patient, . . ."

Some dogs of the time were whistleblowers, calling out the "evils" and "abuse of animals" at the newly formed dog shows. Others wrote their own poems.

> **I hate to walk alone—**
> **my eyes grow very dim;**
> **I'm hard of hearing, too—a fly**
> **Might knock me down, so weak am I**
> **In ev'ry trembling limb.**

Today's dog writers are more often found on the Internet.

Go on Instagram and you'll find dogs everywhere. Lots of the pictures come with captions describing what the dog is (so they say) thinking about. A French bulldog, dressed in striped pajamas, sits up in bed with plump pillows, the day's newspaper, and a plate of croissants. "Best

ALEXANDRA HOROWITZ

slumber party ever!" the caption says. It's meant to be the dog's voice. Oh, and it's meant to sell a particular brand of bottled water, the one the dog is clutching between her paws. (Ha! No dog *I've* ever met . . .)

Instagram dogs model clothes. They sell everything from cleaning products to collars. Many of them have agents. All of the captions and thought bubbles provided for these dogs are another kind of speech—not to the dog, but *for* the dog. Humans provide words for what they want to pretend the dogs are thinking.

We do something similar with other people at times. If someone isn't able to speak, another person sometimes talks for them. One toddler grabs at another's toy, and his mother speaks up: "Oh, he's wondering if you'll share your toy," she explains. A preschool teacher might do the same thing for a student: "You didn't like it when Dina pushed you. You want her to keep her hands to herself." Normally, people with power (a parent, a teacher, a boss) tend to speak up for those with less power (a child, a student, an employee).

And people talk for their dogs. Of a dog lying down at the vet's: "Oh, I'm so tired, I just have to lie down here." Waiting nervously for the vet's exam: "We aren't going to like this at all." We comment for our dogs: We make requests; we report their moods and hopes and fears.

A lot of the time, the sentences we make up for our dogs sound very human—as if our dogs think just like we do. They probably don't. Dogs aren't just small humans in furry coats. Their brains are not just like our brains, and their thoughts are not just like our thoughts.

But when we speak for dogs, we are at least making some kind of an effort to understand their point of view. We try to figure out what they might be thinking and feeling—and by doing so, we have to admit that they have thoughts and feelings that are worth wondering about.

Monologue with Dog

When we talk to dogs, we don't talk the way we would speak to someone of our own age. We don't talk exactly the way we'd speak to very young children, either. We don't even expect a response. So who are we really talking to?

I think the answer is: *Ourselves*. When we talk to our dogs, it's as if our private speech, the conversation we're always having with ourselves in our own heads, has slipped out.

This talking-to-ourselves isn't silly or useless. If we talk through problems out loud, it actually helps to solve them. It also helped all of us first learn a language. Even so, the language we use inside our own heads isn't exactly like what we use when we talk to other people. We use short phrases and quick comments that might not make sense to anybody else. But we understand what we mean.

This is how we talk to our dogs: as if they were inside our own heads.

ALEXANDRA HOROWITZ

And in some ways they are in our minds, of course. We think about our dogs all the time. We hope for them, are concerned for them, and care for them. We narrate our thoughts while we watch them, and their thoughts while they accompany us. Of course, it's in all our heads—only, some of us let the words escape through our mouths.

I've walked around for years, listening to people talk to their dogs, and listening to myself talk to my own. Much of what people say to dogs is nonsense or silly, and we feel as if they are in on the joke. We know they won't respond to us, but we still include them in the conversation.

As we talk to them, we let our dogs in on our secrets. They hear our private thoughts. And according to one survey, two-thirds of pet owners say the same thing to their dogs every day: *I love you.* Even the simple sound of our voice expresses that love.

Now you know: If you pass me on the sidewalk, I might be listening. If you're waiting with your dog at the vet's, I might just be scribbling down what you say.

Please don't let it stop you from talking to your dog.

It's the moment when we are at our most human, and we wear it well.

CHAPTER 6

THE TROUBLE WITH BREEDS

🐾 🐾 🐾 🐾 🐾 🐾 🐾 🐾 🐾 🐾 🐾 🐾 🐾 🐾 🐾

"His stature is dignified, his expression pensive ... (He is) rectangular in shape ... a gentle, loyal and affectionate dog ... An intelligent and independent thinker, he displays determination and a strong sense of purpose while at work. A dog of dignity ..."

(Clumber spaniel breed standard)

🐾 🐾 🐾 🐾 🐾 🐾 🐾 🐾 🐾 🐾 🐾 🐾 🐾 🐾 🐾

Picture a dog. Are you thinking of a golden retriever, a beagle, a Chihuahua? Most likely the dog in your imagination looks like one particular breed. Most dogs in the world aren't purebred dogs, but specific breeds are what we often think of first when we think of "dogs."

The purebred dogs we know today are here because of what is called selective breeding, or artificial selection. People picked the dogs they liked best and let them have puppies. Then they picked the puppies they liked best and let *them* have puppies. And so on and so on and so on.

The result is that we have dogs who are excellent at retrieving game, dogs who are excellent at herding sheep, dogs who are taller than many young children, and dogs who can fit in a teacup. All are members of a single species: dogs. Yet they are astonishingly different—because we have made them that way.

When people meet a dog on the sidewalk, we love to try to figure out her breed. "What breed is your dog?" is a common question. If your dog is a purebred, you can simply say so. "Labrador retriever;" "Chow;" "English sheepdog." If your dog is a mix of two purebred parents, that is an easy answer too. "Goldendoodle" for a dog whose parents were a golden retriever and a standard poodle. If your dog is a true mutt (also called a mix or a mixed breed or a mongrel), you can get creative. Most dog people love to guess the combination of breeds that created that adorable mutt tail, those short legs with the big head, or that panting smile. One shelter in Costa Rica invented a unique breed name for each mixed-breed dog in its care: "Bunnytailed Scottish Shepterrier;" "Freckled Terrierhuahua;" "Fire-Tailed Border Cocker."

Some dog owners aren't content to guess. They find themselves taking a cotton swab and rubbing it between their dog's cheek and gum until it is soaked with saliva. Once they send that saliva to a laboratory, it can be tested to give you an idea of what breeds came together to make up your dog.

But what does such an answer actually tell us?

Thinking of dogs only in terms of their breeds can limit what we come to see and understand about them. It can even be dangerous—not just for us, but for our dogs.

People have become so interested in breeding certain kinds of dogs—huge dogs, tiny dogs, dogs with flat faces, dogs with interesting colors—that we've ended up causing harm to the animals we love. What the breed world has been guided by was not specifically a healthy, happy dog, but a trophy handed out by a judge at a dog show.

The Dog Library

"Not a fragile dog, but is also a dog with class and grace. The attitude is noble and somewhat aloof, and the expression of the dark eyes is gentle and melancholy."
(Sloughi breed standard)

On a warm September day, I head into an office building in New York City. On the fourth floor, the elevator doors open to a carpeted lobby lined with marble pillars. On top of every pillar is a small statue under glass, each of a different breed of dog. As I turn down a hallway, I spot nearly a hundred small dog heads, tiny statues on top of walking sticks, jostling for a treat or pat from a passerby.

The hallway opens into a large room. There are dogs

everywhere. I pet a small statue of a snuffling basset hound, stare at oil paintings of setters and fox terriers, and meet Belgrave Joe, the original fox terrier, who died in 1888. His skeleton, complete with curved tail, has been preserved in a glass case.

This is the library of the American Kennel Club. In front of me are dozens of stud books. Each lists all the registered members of a particular breed of dog—over fifty million members over the years. When the American Kennel Club began in 1884, dogs were sometimes mated with dogs outside the breed. A bulldog might be bred with a terrier, say. Her puppies and their puppies might still be counted as bulldogs. This is no longer allowed. Today, each breed is a club with a very limited membership. To have a place in one of these books, a purebred dog must have a purebred mother and father. The dog's owners could trace their dog's parents, grandparents, great-grandparents, and so on to one of the earliest "founding dogs" listed in the stud books. That's what made them "pure" (or so it was thought): they were unmixed with other kinds of dogs.

Bred for Function

Well before the American Kennel Club and other organizations began to keep records on the breeding of dogs, dogs came in many types. Early humans wanted dogs who would chase deer that the humans wanted to eat, or who could bring back a bird that a hunter had killed, or who would bark ferociously when a stranger approached. Perhaps these early humans chose dogs who simply looked like they'd be good at the jobs they needed to do. A slim, long-legged dog might be good at chasing prey. A stocky dog with powerful jaws might be good at scaring off intruders.

Medieval tapestries show lean, pantherlike dogs keeping pace with horses during hunts. A painting of a wedding scene from 1434 includes a small dog with the head of a Pomeranian and the body of a terrier, who was most likely a lapdog.

The first known lists of types of dogs, published in 1486, includes Grehoun (greyhounds), Mastiff, and Spanyel (spaniels). Nearly a hundred years later, another list described terrars (terriers) who chased foxes and badgers; Bloudhoundes and other hounds who tracked prey for hunters; and the Spaniel-gentle or Comforter dog, a lapdog for ladies "to play and dally withal." Other dogs were listed: the Tynckers Curre (tinker's dog) who carried a tinker's mending supplies; the Turnespete (turnspit) dogs, who ran on a wheel to turn a spit over the fire; Mooners, who bayed at the moon; and Daunsers (dancers), performing dogs who did "many pretty trickes" to music.

Does this mean that a mastiff is the oldest breed in the world? Or a spaniel? Or a greyhound? The truth is that no dog breed we recognize today can honestly claim to be the most ancient one that exists. Some purebred dogs descriptions say that their breed existed before all the rest, but in

fact breeds, as we think about them today, are a modern invention.

Those early lists of dogs describe types, not breeds. They cataloged dogs by the jobs they did. A "grehoun" from 1486 might have been slim and fast; a mastiff was probably large and stocky. But they weren't necessarily related to the greyhounds or mastiffs of today, because they weren't being bred by owners committed to mating greyhounds only with greyhounds and mastiffs only to other mastiffs. That's what "purebred" means, and it wasn't something that existed until about 130 years ago.

What early dog owners wanted was to get puppies

who were good at the work they needed the dogs to do. Different types would have formed more or less naturally, as people chose dogs who looked fast, tough, or cuddly, and then went on to allow the ones they liked to have puppies—who were fast, tough, or cuddly as well.

So if an English gentleman in the 1800s with a pack of foxhounds happened to see a dog he admired, he might ask if he could breed that dog with one of his own. Maybe the puppies would be even better hunters—quicker, stronger, with a good baying call and a keen nose for foxes. Perhaps he'd even breed a coonhound father and a beagle mother, hoping to end up with puppies who combined the best traits of both.

Today the most common breeding of dogs is not for their ability to do a job. Most of the people who register their dogs with the American Kennel Club aren't looking for hounds to chase foxes or rabbits across the country, or shepherds to guard sheep, or terriers to hunt rats. Today's dogs are primarily bred for looks. A purebred bulldog is a dog who looks like the bulldog's "breed standard," a description of how the breed is supposed to look. That's the whole point.

Purebreeding Begins

"He is an attractive dog of handy size."
(Welsh springer spaniel breed standard)

This change from breeding dogs to do a job to breeding dogs who look a certain way started in the late 1800s. In

1889, a breeder chose a dog called Horand von Grafrath to begin creating what he hoped would be a perfect sheepherding dog. His owner described Horand as having "beautiful lines." He was "clean and sinewy in build" and "one live wire." And he had "the straightforward nature of a gentleman with a boundless zest for living."

Horand is the first named German shepherd, and if you own a purebred German shepherd with papers, your dog's ancestry can be traced back through the years to this dog.

An interest in breeding dogs to look a certain way came along with a new fashion in those days: dog shows. It was already common to have shows where examples of farm animals (pigs, chickens, cows, horses) were judged and prizes were given. Dog shows became part of this tradition. The first was held in Newcastle-upon-Tyne, England, in 1859.

The new dog shows were an instant hit. Some had more than a thousand dogs. Breeding and showing dogs became known as "the dog fancy," and owners were called "fanciers." Shows began to offer money prizes for the winners, and some owners were so eager to win that they cheated by dyeing their dogs' coats and trimming ears or tails to the correct shape and size with scissors.

To provide some order, a Kennel Club was formed in London in 1873, and the American Kennel Club in Philadelphia in 1884. These clubs laid down rules for which dogs could be considered purebred and which could not. To belong, a dog needed a registered name that could go in the stud book and a family record showing purebred ancestors. The clubs also held their own dogs shows, and continue to do so today. At the Kennel Club's Crufts dog show, held in England, thousands of owners arrive with their dogs to compete for the title of "Best in Show." And the United States has the Westminster Kennel Club dog show in New York City.

Back in 1859, at the first dog show, the best pointer was

ALEXANDRA HOROWITZ

"by Lord Derby's Bang out of his Dora." (In other words, the winner's father was Bang, the mother was Dora, and both mother and father were owned by Lord Derby.) But what made Bang and Dora's puppy such a winner? How did the judges decide which dog was the best?

Breed Standards and Mutts

To answer these questions, people who all owned the same breed of dog developed clubs. The breed "fanciers", as show-dog enthusiasts are called, also came up with standards for each breed. In 1892, a bulldog breed club decided that the best bulldogs should have a lower jaw that stuck out, a face "as short as possible," and skin "deeply and closely wrinkled." As for the skull, "the larger the better." The shoulders needed to be "broad, slanting and deep" to bear the weight of a wide chest—even though the wide chest tended to make it hard for the bulldog to walk normally. But as for a light-colored nose, called a "Dudley nose"? That was, for some reason, unacceptable.

Bulldogs were not the only ones who came to have standards: all purebreeds do. The cocker spaniel should be twice as long "from nip of nose to root of tail" as they are tall at the shoulder. The mastiff's head is supposed to be exactly two thirds as wide as long. The English pug breed standard insists that pugs have a short, square muzzle; a round head; strong, straight legs; and a stocky body. Their coats should be glossy, with "large and deep" wrinkles. As for the tail, "the double curl is perfection."

Other kinds of dogs—those who did not live up to these standards—were not considered perfection. As standards developed for different breeds, people began to express scorn for dogs who did not live up to these standards—for those dogs who were not purebreds.

One veterinarian in the early 1900s, for instance, claimed that dogs who were not purebred "can never hope to equal the true, pureblooded animals with their generations of unmixed blood." The owner of Horand, the first official German shepherd, said much the same thing. "Creatures of pure blood, where by proper breeding all unevennesses have been eliminated, far surpass all mongrels," he declared.

Purebred dogs were better, these people thought, not because they did a job better. It was because they looked a certain way. And they were thought to be better than mixed-breed dogs just because, well, they were. "Mutts," "mongrels," "curs"—these were the words people used to describe dogs who were not purebred. They were not intended as a compliment. ("Mutt" is actually short for "muttonhead," which isn't a kind thing to say of dogs, sheep, or people. Still, today, I don't mean anything bad when I use "mutt"; in fact, I use it to mean a kind of mixed-breed dog I like.)

It wasn't just that purebreds were thought to be better dogs. Owners of purebreds were thought to be better people. "Nobody now who is anybody," one magazine for dog owners declared in 1890, "can afford to be followed about by a mongrel dog."

Before the mid-1850s, there were no purebred dogs. There were various *types* of dogs, doing different jobs, which were then mixed to make breeds. Today, there are more than two hundred breeds recognized by the American Kennel Club. When humans domesticated wolves to create dogs, we changed the species for the first time. To create breeds that we think are cute, impressive, or beautiful, we changed the species again.

These days, people sometimes don't just think about whether they should get "a dog." They think, "What *breed* suits me?" A pit bull? A Shih Tzu? A slobbery, loveable Labrador? A German shepherd like Rin-Tin-Tin or a Dalmatian like the ones in *101 Dalmatians* or a golden retriever like the funny one you follow on Instagram?

We live in a world where you can answer an ad in the newspaper for "Collie puppies, finest breeding," or "Toy French Poodle puppies: snow white, long silky coats, long ears, and jet-black eyes." You can also drive to a breeder and get exactly what you want.

There's the trouble.

CHAPTER 7

MORE TROUBLE WITH BREEDS

🐾 🐾 🐾 🐾 🐾 🐾 🐾 🐾 🐾 🐾 🐾 🐾

In 2003, a Pekingese named Danny competed at the Crufts dog show. He raced around the ring, panting, his tongue curled up in his mouth. His large, bulging eyes darted frantically. While he was in the show ring, his owner had to put him on top of an ice pack, because his body was overheating. He couldn't breathe in enough air to stay cool.

He won Best in Show.

🐾 🐾 🐾 🐾 🐾 🐾 🐾 🐾 🐾 🐾 🐾 🐾

All dogs of a breed are meant to look a particular way. That's the whole point. The closer each dog comes to the standards laid out by a breed club, the better, as far as the dog fancy is concerned.

Owners carefully choose which bulldogs or pointers or pugs should mate, trying to produce puppies who look just like they should. And they often do more. To make their dogs match breed standards, owners may even need to put them through surgery.

In the earliest shows, owners might have taken a scissors to their dog's ears to give them a better chance of winning a dog show. Today, the standards for twenty breeds (Dobermans and Great Danes included) still say that ears can or should be cropped. This means taking off two thirds of the dog's ear—the soft, lovely flap that folds downward. The remaining stub is splinted and bandaged so that it will stand upright.

Sixty-two other breeds (cocker spaniels and Rottweilers among them) must have their tails cropped, according to the breed standards. This means amputating a dog's tail when she is still a very young puppy—a painful operation that also cuts off one of a dog's best ways to communicate.

There's no real reason that short tails are better than long ones, or spiky triangular ears are better than floppy ones. Dogs suffer through these painful, bewildering surgeries only so that they can look the way humans think they should look.

Inbreeding

But surgery alone can't make all the dogs in a breed match perfectly in size, weight, and color. Every Sussex spaniel, for example, is supposed to have a nose between three and three and a half inches long. The Gordon setter's nose should be exactly one inch longer.

> **"Closely set eyes are to be faulted . . . A pointed muzzle is not desirable . . . A dish-shaped muzzle is a fault . . . Too many wrinkles in the forehead is a fault . . . A spotted nose is not desirable. A flesh colored nose disqualifies."**
> (German shorthaired pointer breed standard)

There is only one way to get dogs who look like this much alike: ensure that only a small group of dogs mate with each other. This ends up meaning that brothers mate with sisters. Parents mate with their pups.

When close relatives mate with each other, it's called inbreeding. Serious health problems start appearing more often among inbred dogs. They are far more likely to have fewer puppies, and their puppies are likely to have shorter lifespans.

The Rhodesian ridgeback has been bred for a stripe of bristly hair all the way down the dog's back. But the same genes that create this unique ruff of fur leads to skin and nerve problems. Dalmatians are bred for their white coats with black spots. They are also more likely to be deaf and to have painful problems urinating.

People aren't actually setting out to breed dogs who will have short lives or be deaf or suffer from painful problems with their skin. They're trying to breed dogs who will have a bristly stripe of fur or pretty black spots. But even though the same health problems will keep coming up, over and over, the dogs are inbred anyway.

When I asked a vet which breed had suffered the most from inbreeding, she did not hesitate. "Bulldogs," she said.

If you compare a picture of an English bulldog from 1866 with one from today, it's hard to believe you are looking at the same breed. Those bulldogs from a century and a half ago had actual faces. Their muzzles stuck out, as most dogs' do.

No longer. Today's bulldogs look almost as if they've run into something face-first. The nose is jammed backward. The jaw is thrust forward. Folds of skin drape like curtains. The eyes bulge out. Their bodies are stocky and thick, their legs overly short.

Bulldog heads are huge. The breed standards for the

bulldog in 1892 stated that the dog's skull should be "very large—the larger, the better." Today, bulldog puppies have such big heads that they cannot be born naturally. In most cases, a vet must deliver them by surgery, in what is called a caesarean section.

Because of the way their skin folds and droops, bulldogs often get skin infections and sores. Their bulging eyes cause their eyelids to roll in or out, damaging the sensitive parts of the eye. Their short legs and wide bodies mean they waddle awkwardly and struggle to run—and sometimes to walk.

Bulldogs even struggle to breathe.

Breeding the dogs for short, flat muzzles means that, over time, the shape of their skull has been changed. Because of these changes, there is simply not enough room for air in the dog's nose and throat. "It's like breathing through a straw," the vet said, describing the way bulldogs and other flat-faced dogs, such as pugs, have to struggle to pull enough air into their lungs.

One way that dogs keep their bodies at a regular temperature is by breathing. That's why they pant in the heat. Many short-nosed dogs can't draw in enough air to keep their bodies from overheating. Some need surgery simply to be able to breathe in comfort.

These dogs are suffering because people find their flattened faces cute to look at. (People tend to find animals with flatter faces—without long noses—adorable. This may be because flatter faces and big eyes remind people of human babies, and most people can't help but find that kind of face endearing.) But it's not a good enough reason for a dog to live a life of snuffling, snorting, and struggling to draw a decent breath.

It's not only flat-faced dogs like bulldogs and pugs who suffer from humans' desire to make their dogs look a certain way. Remember Horand, the first official German shepherd? A photograph of him shows a strong, sturdy dog with a bushy tail draping casually behind him. You can see he's a German shepherd, but he'd never win Best in Breed today.

Today's German shepherds look quite different. They've been bred over many years for long, sloping backs and short legs. This causes painful problems with their hip joints that can actually cripple some dogs. Other breeds suffer in similar ways. The Cavalier King Charles spaniel has a skull so small that the brain can swell, which is extremely painful. Giant dogs like Great Danes suffer from hip and bone problems; so do dogs bred to be tiny. Pugs have bulging eyes that can easily be damaged or develop sores. Basset hounds struggle with back problems.

These are not simply dogs who are unlucky. These are dogs who are suffering because of choices humans made when we decided which dogs should have puppies and which shouldn't.

Unreasonable Expectations

Humans breed dogs for looks—and that causes terrible problems. But we also assume that dogs of a certain breed will reliably act a certain way, and that is a problem of its own.

We often think that all purebred dogs have similar personalities. Retrievers are thought of as gentle. Dobermans are assumed to be fierce. Advertisements for breeds, and breed standards, claim that if you get a purebred dog, you will get a dog whose behavior is predictable. That you will know how that dog will act. But this doesn't hold up in real life.

If you look at a pile of puppies just a few weeks old, they do seem to be very much alike at first. They are squeaking, snuffling, tumbling fur puddles. But then one pup breaks away and aims for your outstretched finger. Another notices a shoelace dangling off a sneaker and fumbles after it. A third burrows into their mother's belly. A fourth climbs on the third. One has a pink nose; one has a white tip to his tail. Each is different. Each is unique. And every moment they will grow more into themselves.

When scientists have tested dogs' behavior, they have found something surprising: members of the same breed are as different from each other as they are from members of other breeds. In other words, two border collies can be as different from each other as one might be from a Yorkshire terrier. Dogs of the same breed can be very different: one easygoing; another lively. Some are friendly with strangers; some prefer their own people. Some follow every command; some come only when they feel like coming.

Why? Well, easy: Each is an individual. Just like you, each dog has his or her own personality. Your behavior can't be predicted by your genes, and neither can a dog's.

There is one exception to this general rule. Breeds do tend to react alike to certain things that catch their attention. Any dog can see and smell a rat, but most terriers (also called ratters) cannot rest until they've dug that rat out from a hole. My own dogs will notice sheep, come close to them, wonder at them, and sniff them enthusiastically. But they don't do what almost any border collie will do—lock their gaze on the sheep (this is called "showing eye"), stalk closer, and drive those sheep where they want them to go.

Hounds bay, pointers point, and retrievers (usually) retrieve. Breeds that were developed to do a particular job—fetch game, herd sheep, hunt rats—tend to behave in ways that still match that job. If retrievers don't have birds to bring back to their owners, a tennis ball will do. If herding dogs can't find any sheep, they might try to herd nearby skateboarders.

But predicting how dogs might react to a flapping bird or a soaring tennis ball is far from the same as predicting a dog's personality. Still, many breeders and breed guides claim to do this. The standard for the golden retriever declares that the breed is "friendly, reliable and trustworthy." Maybe your parents chose a golden retriever for your family because the website of the American Kennel Club announces that these dogs are "good with children."

Indeed, I've known many exceptionally friendly golden retrievers. They greet people enthusiastically. They very nearly smile. But if you assume that all of these dogs are friendly at all times, you may not notice if a golden retriever is getting frustrated or nervous, and that can lead to trouble.

Suppose parents think that they don't need to keep an eye on a dog around a toddler because a website says this dog will be "good with children"? Those parents are setting themselves up for problems. If a young child snatches a dog's favorite toy or tries to ride him like a pony, a bite may soon follow. And that's a situation that might not have happened if an owner wasn't convinced that all golden retrieves are friendly no matter what.

One study compared the reports of aggressive behavior of golden retrievers with other dogs who are sometimes thought of as "dangerous"—Dobermans, Rottweilers, pit bulls. It found no difference between the breeds at all.

The idea that every golden retriever is always calm can have serious consequences. And the opposite is true. Very often it happens that people become convinced that an

ALEXANDRA HOROWITZ

entire breed of dogs is untrustworthy—mean, aggressive, dangerous.

Which breed? It changes over time.

"Dangerous" Breeds

In 1876, people were very concerned about a breed known as the Spitz. "He is a tireless and shameless thief," the *New York Times* insisted. It added that the dog "exhibits a perverted skill in obtaining access to forbidden cellars, and in stealing the reserved bones of honest and frugal dogs."

This dangerous, treacherous dog looked a bit like today's Pomeranian and was tiny enough to be tucked into a purse.

The Saint Bernard was also feared and distrusted in the 1800s. So was the dachshund.

Over a century later, a tragedy occurred in the United Kingdom, when an eleven-year-old girl was killed by a pair of Rottweilers. Suddenly all Rottweilers were suspect. Newspapers called them "terrorists on four legs," and "devil dogs." Owners of Rottweilers were scolded in public for walking their dogs. Lawmakers decided to protect citizens from dangerous dogs with something new: laws that banned entire breeds, called breed-specific legislation.

The UK law banned four breeds: Japanese Tosa, Fila Brasiliero, Dogo Argentino, and pit bulls. Oddly, Rottweilers were off the hook.

Under these laws, dogs who are declared dangerous can be taken away from their owners and euthanized (a way of saying "humanely killed"; sometimes people say "put to sleep"). Or they may be required to be leashed and muzzled at all times, even if they have never shown any aggressive behavior at all.

Doberman pinschers, German shepherds, Chow Chows, and many other breeds have been banned in various places at different times. But today, the dogs who are banned most often are pit bulls.

It wasn't always so. Pit bulls have appeared three times on the cover of *Life* magazine—not because they were frightening, but because they were considered adorable. President Teddy Roosevelt had a pit bull in the White House—although he did chase the French ambassador up a tree.

Today, to many, pit bulls are no longer considered cute. And there have indeed been times where pit bulls have bitten people and even, in a few cases, killed children. (These are sad and rare events that can happen with any breed.) News reports tended to play up the violence of horrible events like these but neglected to explain if there were important details, like a toddler left alone with a dog, or that the dog was abused and starved.

People, it seemed, were not interested in hearing why one particular pit bull might have acted aggressively at one particular time. As humans often do, we generalized:

ALEXANDRA HOROWITZ

started to see all pit bulls as like the one pit bull we read about. So people assumed that all pit bulls are the same and all are dangerous. Once again, people were quick to believe that all members of a breed act alike.

One trouble with this idea is there isn't actually a breed called a pit bull.

There is an American pit bull terrier, an American Staffordshire terrier, a Staffordshire bull terrier, and an American bully. Some laws declare that any dog who has any of these breeds as ancestors, even distant ancestors, is a pit bull.

But mostly "pit bull" doesn't have a real meaning. It's just used to describe any dog with short hair, a blocky head, a stocky body, a streaky coat of brown or tan, and maybe a white star on the chest. A dog who looks like this may have some of the four "pit bull breeds" in her, or she may not. There's simply no way to tell by just looking— and even experts are often wrong when they guess a breed by looks alone!

Even if you could be sure which dog is a pit bull (whatever that may mean), there is no actual proof that pit bulls or dogs with some kind of pit bull ancestry are more aggressive than any others. And there's zero proof, as well, that laws banning ownership of a particular breed of dogs—any breed—do a thing to reduce dog bites and attacks. One study looked at bans that affected thirteen different breeds of dogs. It found that there were slightly *more* dog bites recorded after a ban than before.

When we think that all dogs of a same breed are sure to look and act the same, we pass laws and make rules that don't keep people safe, but that treat harmless dogs as if they are deadly dangerous. (At the same time, we sometimes forget that breeds we think of as harmless can be dangerous as well.) The truth is that any dog with teeth can bite—a pit bull, a golden retriever, a Shih Tzu, a mutt. Looking at a dog's breed tells you very little about how aggressive they may be.

And the breeds that we think of as dangerous are actually not the ones who bite most often. One study looked at which breeds of dogs actually do act most aggressively. It wasn't pit bulls, or Rottweilers, or mastiffs.

So which breed is it?

Dachshunds—the cute, short-legged small dogs who used to sometimes be called "hot dogs" for their extra-long bodies.

(Of course not all dachshunds are aggressive. As with all breeds, each dog is different.)

Changing Breeding

We cannot continue breeding dogs as we have been doing. When we mate closely related dogs, hoping to produce puppies who look a way that pleases us, we harm those dogs terribly. When we think of every member of a breed as identical, we stop seeing dogs for who and what they really are. That harms them in another way.

The simplest way to stop all this? Change breeding. What if people couldn't make new dogs for money? What if they couldn't buy dogs from breeders who sell hundreds or thousands of puppies every year? Breeding this many dogs at a time can't help but mean that the dogs and puppies are treated like products, like things, instead of like living individuals with their own needs and feelings. Right now, breeding dogs is a business, practiced to make a profit. If it weren't, there would be less incentive to design dogs for consumers.

Future owners can do their part, too, by, for instance, not buying dogs from pet stores. All pet stores buy their dogs from puppy mills. Puppy mills are high-volume breeders; puppies are often kept in unsanitary conditions; they are not allowed to spend enough time with people or with other dogs, sometimes not even giving them enough food or medical care.

Humane societies and shelter workers have the right idea when they say "Adopt, don't shop." If you simply walk into a shelter, where barks ring through the hallways, you'll quickly see how true this is. Each face peering out pleads with you. Dogs lying curled around themselves, or a litter of puppies curled around each other, melt my heart.

Imagine if we decided to stop breeding any dogs at all until each of these shelter dogs finds a home.

But even if breeding continues, it can be improved. We

can try to make sure people breed dogs for best *health*, not just good looks. And in the meantime, if you don't get a shelter dog, it's best to find a breeder who raises no more than one or two litters a year. Puppies like this are more likely to be kept with their mothers, who you should be able to meet; they might live in the house; they see people all the time, and are part of their family—until they become part of yours. They have a way better start than puppies born in a puppy mill.

Another way to make life better for our dogs would be to stop breeding inbred dogs, and start crossbreeding. Breed a golden retriever with a standard poodle, a cocker spaniel with a Labrador, a husky with a beagle. And breed their puppies with dogs of different breeds as well. Don't worry, everyone—crossbred dogs like these will still be fantastic. Look at mutts, who are already crossbred many times over. They are adorable, loyal, friendly—and unique.

Each one is their own dog, just as each of us is our own person.

CHAPTER 8

THE SCIENTIFIC PROCESS AS PRACTICED AT HOME WATCHING DOGS ON A THURSDAY EVENING

A scientist spends her days working with the scientific process, a way to solve problems and figure out the answers to questions. You can use it to figure out why an

apple falls from a tree branch to the ground or how old the universe is or whether dogs rely more on their sense of sight or their sense of smell.

It goes like this:

- Observe the world around you. Ask a question about something you want to understand.
- Come up with a hypothesis: an educated guess.
- Consider your hypothesis. Is it the only possible answer? Is there another explanation that might make more sense?
- Come up with a revised hypothesis. Or two. Or three. Or four.

ALEXANDRA HOROWITZ

- Design an experiment specifically to test your final hypothesis.
- Run the experiment, gather your data, and take a look at them.
- Use the data from your experiment to draw a conclusion. Is your hypothesis true? False? Mostly true but a little bit false?

In my lab, the scientific process might look like this:

HYPHOTHESIS: When dogs put on a guilty look (with their heads down, ears back, tails low and wagging fast), it's because they've done something wrong.

We think we can tell what our dogs are feeling. We say a dog with a treat in his mouth looks happy. A dog who's just dragged a big stick out of a pond looks proud. A dog who can tell you're about to leave for school looks sad.

But are we right about what the dog is feeling? Does a proud/happy/sad look on the outside of the dog match up to the feeling on the inside?

What about a feeling of guilt?

A really common thing we say about dogs is that they "look guilty" when they've done something we think is wrong. Owners say that when they come home, for instance, and see this look on their dog's face, they know that the dog has done something the owners don't approve of—like getting into the garbage. But do dogs actually feel guilty?

I got interested in thinking about this after reading a newspaper story about a Doberman pinscher named Barney who was left alone to guard a very valuable collection: all of Elvis Presley's teddy bears. (Elvis was a wildly popular singer who also had a really large collection of teddy bears when he was alive.) Well, in the morning someone came in and discovered Barney lying peacefully among hundreds of mangled, chewed teddy bears, many with limbs off and their stuffing flung around the room.

It was a very funny story, really. I think the lesson is: Don't leave a dog in charge of a collection of soft toys (which look just like "chew toys" we give them to chew on!). But someone looked at the photo of Barney with a policeman surveying the scene and said (of Barney), "Well, he looks like he feels sorry for what he did. He knows it was wrong."

• I gave my hypothesis some thought. Barney certainly looked ashamed, lying there among the headless, armless, eyeless teddy bears. But is looking ashamed necessarily the same as feeling ashamed? Can I tell for sure what Barney is feeling by the way Barney is looking?

• I came up with a revised hypothesis: Dogs' guilty look isn't about their having done something wrong.

Since so many owners feel sure that their dogs' guilty look came up when they'd gotten into the garbage or eaten food on the counter, this seemed like a good place to start thinking about a study about dogs' guilty look. I remember reading another scientist's suggestion that dogs looked guilty when they were just *around* strewn garbage on the floor or a half-eaten dinner—even when they hadn't eaten the dinner or strewn the garbage themselves.

Maybe it could be that dogs put on that look not because of what they did (or didn't do), but because of something happening later. In particular, something happening to them at the moment that their owners see them.

• I came up with another revised hypothesis: Dogs' guilty looks are a response to their owners.

Well, who is there at that moment they are discovered with the garbage around them? We are. We see the garbage, look at the dog, and put our hands on our hips and begin to say: "What did you do . . . ?"

• I designed an experiment. (You can find out more about this experiment in Chapter Nine of my book *Inside of a Dog* if you're curious.) The idea was to get a dog to either obey or disobey a command ("Don't eat this treat left on the floor!") when their owner was out of the room. When the owner came back, she greeted the dog happily if he'd obeyed, or scolded him if he'd disobeyed. But sometimes I told the owners that their dogs had obeyed, when they hadn't! Or that they hadn't obeyed, when they had. How much of that guilty look did the dogs show— more when they were guilty? Or more when their owners *thought* they were guilty?

• I ran the experiment with fourteen dogs whose owners had volunteered for the study. You know what I found? Dogs didn't look any more guilty when they'd eaten the forbidden treat than when they hadn't. But they *did* look more guilty when their owners thought they had eaten it.

• I came to a conclusion: It is not doing something wrong that makes a dog look guilty. Dogs don't automatically know what's right and wrong in your house. But they do learn very quickly that when we look angry, or we start saying, "Finnegan, did you do this . . . ?" it's a good time to put on a really cute look. Their "guilty" look is not a response to something a dog is feeling. It's a response to us.

That is how the scientific process plays out in a typical study in my lab. At home, my mind works in the same way. It begins simply enough. I'm minding my own business, and suddenly my brain comes up with a question or even a hypothesis. Usually this happens after milling about the house with dogs, gazing out the window at a bunch of dogs outside, or staring vaguely at some data about dogs I've brought home from the lab. Happily, this means that most of my ideas are about dogs.

I've gone on to test many of the hypotheses I've come up with like this, and some have even turned out to be true. I've figured out that, when dogs pick a person to come close to, they prefer one who has a lot of treats to one who's been fair in handing out treats equally to every pup. I've found out that dogs can notice when the smell of their own bodies has changed. I've hypothesized that dogs can tell time by noticing how the smell of their owners gets fainter as the day goes on.

Some of my hypotheses have led me to discover things I hadn't thought of. We found out that dogs can smell the difference between a large amount of something and a smaller amount of that same thing, for example. Our lab discovered that people like dog faces with larger eyes and mouths that seem to smile, but those who say that they're not "animal people" don't care. And we've seen that people roughhousing with their dogs show more positive emotions than people who are playing fetch.

But sometimes, I have to admit, when I'm at home watching dogs, I don't always follow the scientific process exactly. Sometimes I skip the experiments and play around with the hypothesis and find myself in some unexpected and even silly places.

🐾 🐾 🐾

HYPOTHESIS: The dog is an animal.

This seems very likely. The food that goes into the dog, the pee and poop that come out, the way the dogs sleeps and wakes, the eyes, ears, mouth, the tail—everything points toward "animal." I feel pretty solid with this one.

• Let's consider the hypothesis.

We couldn't be more horrified if we found a dog in a zoo—which is, after all, a place that houses animals. Also, this morning in a coffee shop I saw a Labradoodle sitting on a high stool, wearing a quilted winter jacket, and gazing deep into the eyes of the person next to him. The dog's owner let him lick the foam on her cappuccino.

• Revised hypothesis: The dog is a person.

After all, my dear friend knit me a lovely pair of gloves as a Christmas gift. And she also knit an angora sweater, with cable stitching, for the dog. So not only is the dog a person, she is a worthier person than I.

But on the other hand, dogs seem to be getting away with not having much of a job. And they don't go to school, either. Still, you can't call them slackers. They never really watch TV or surf the web. Instead of working or studying or going on the Internet, they spend their walks with their noses on the ground. At home, they mostly lie around listening for intruders.

• Second revised hypothesis: The dog is a wolf.

There's some evidence for this one. But it's very, very old. I'm not sure we can trust it.

• Conclusion: The dog is a spy.

Why, the other day I caught Finnegan seeming to "sleep on the sofa," but actually peering at me from the corner of his eyes. And when I woke up this morning he was sitting by the bed staring at me. The notebook I keep by my bedside had been chewed to shreds. A spy for sure.

🐾 🐾 🐾

HYPOTHESIS: A dog is man's best friend.

It seems so to me. Surely, my two perfect dogs are my

best friends. One of them found my lost datebook for me. The other smiles when he sees me. Both of them are never cruel. They're almost always cheerful. They never judge me for my faults.

• Consider the hypothesis.

As I move off the sofa so that the dogs can have more room, I can't help but wonder, though, if they are at all cunning. After all, I buy the dogs their own bagels. I pay more for their vet bills than my doctor bills. Because of them, I have pockets filled with dried salmon. Our family doesn't usually travel far because we can't bring the dogs with us. We scoop their poop up in bags as if it were precious. We live in a constant haze of dog fur.

• Revised hypothesis: Dog are actually just manipulating us to get what they want.

Since we adopted a cat, I have seen that dogs and cats are actually quite similar—only the cat doesn't wag when we get home, gaze at us adoringly, and promptly respond when spoken to. Sure, she cozies up to every guest to the house, jumping on their laps and relentlessly purring and rubbing against them. But after I've watched her do this over and over, it begins to look less like affection and more like a way of getting what the cat wants: a warm, soft spot to sit.

Now that I think about it, I noticed Finnegan making a noise suspiciously like purring when I rubbed his ears.

• Second revision: Dog is a cat.

Impossible. Dogs would never betray us like that.

- Conclusion: Cats are really dogs who haven't passed the act-like-a-best-friend test.

🐾 🐾 🐾

HYPOTHESIS: Dogs know when you're coming home.

People claim that their dogs can tell when they're about to arrive home. It seems possible. Maybe the dogs know your habits. Maybe they can catch your scent as you start up the front walk. Maybe they are using some sense we have not discovered yet.

- Consider the hypothesis.

If dogs know in advance how long you'll be gone and when you'll return, would they be so bent out of shape when you leave to go down to the basement for three minutes?

- Revised hypothesis: Dogs are just by the front door anyway, just in case you come home.

They figure that they might as well wait there, since after a while you'll be bound to show up. You always have before. But sometimes my dogs aren't by the front door when I open it. Or one dog is there and the other is not.

- Second revision: The first dog is distracting me with a rambunctious greeting while the other finishes buying his favorite toys on the Internet.

Come to think of it, there are a lot of unexplained late-night Amazon purchases on my account. A lot of them seem to involve salmon.

- Conclusion: On the Internet, everyone is a dog.

HYPOTHESIS: Dogs cannot talk.

This seems obvious. We talk to dogs all the time. Thank goodness, they don't answer back.

• Consider the hypothesis.

On the other hand, I've been hearing from dogs all my life. It's just not out loud. When I ask if they want to go out, they tell me they do. When I ask if they want a treat, their answer is clear. When I ask if they're hungry or tired or want to come for a walk or would like some of my sandwich, the answer is yes.

• Revised hypothesis: Dogs know how to say yes, but they don't know how to say no.

But: baths.

Oh. A dog is speaking to me now. He's come to tell me something. Dogs may start subtly, by sitting across the room with their attention aimed at you, but they know that we are pretty bad at speaking dog, and they will continue to yell at us: HEY! HEY! HEY! until we finally turn and look. We are so dense.

Wait, he's saying something. . . .

Dog has told me to stop this.

Such is the fast-and-furious nature of science.

CHAPTER 9

DOG STUFF

That blue-and-orange ball over there? No, not that one; the smaller one. The nubby, muddy one. Right. That one is definitely Finnegan's. Or at least (as he snarls at a dog eyeing it) he seems very certain that it is.

Finn's ball lies on the carpet alongside a dozen other balls—rubbery ones that once had feet and squeakers, before Upton chewed them off. There are also stuffed toys, half-shredded, and some rope-and-chew toys that they're not too fond of. There are dog beds in the bedroom, dog bowls in the kitchen, and leashes, vests, and towels in the entryway.

It's all my dogs'.

It's a cool morning in May when he darts across the sidewalk in front of me. A woman three steps behind him hurries to keep up. He doesn't wait a second before charging through an open door and into a store.

He's wearing a tricolor argyle sweater and has a leather cord with ruby-red jewels on it around his neck. He looks all around, from floor to ceiling, before zeroing in on a cat, hissing, under a shelf.

He's a Jack Russell terrier, and he's just arrived at the pet store.

Your dog probably knows the way to the nearest pet store, no matter if you go there on foot or by car. But pet stores really exist because the people on the other end of the leash want for their pups what they want for themselves: stuff. People love to buy stuff, be given stuff, and own stuff. Stuff for ourselves and stuff for our dogs.

I watch the terrier's exploration of the pet store. After he's done with the cat, he drools into a bin of pigs' ears, mouths a rubber ball, and dashes for the counter where he stands up on his hind legs. For this he earns a small treat, tossed into the air. His tags jingle as he tugs his owner forward. Another dog, a miniature collie, leaps over her taut leash.

Both dogs dart between bins on the floor that hold rawhide treats, rubber chews, and dog food samples. Their owners let their gazes linger on pink, red, blue, and green toys on the shelves at eye height.

If dogs could go online, they could browse these products from the comfort of their monogrammed dog bed at home. The website of one shop, called Canine Styles, features polar-fleece track suits, cashmere sweaters (in red, hot pink, and herringbone), puffer coats, tartan rain jackets, hoodies, tennis dresses, and Hawaiian print "vacation shirts." Once a dog is properly dressed, he can also shop for bone-shaped placemats, plaid bow ties, and a bin to put all of his toys in. He'll probably need one.

Elsewhere online, you can buy a designer "pawbag" that your dog can wear on her collar to match your own designer purse. There are hundreds of colognes, perfumes, and body sprays made for dogs. You can get your dog nail polish or a 100 percent cotton bathrobe (and your own 100 percent cotton bathrobe to match).

When did we decide that animals need cologne or nail polish? How did it come to be that we are buying the food, toys, bathrobes, and purses that we are for our dogs?

Stores for Pets and People

As we've already seen, according to the law, dogs are property. They can't own property themselves. To the law, things cannot own things. But boy, do dogs *own* things.

A little more than a century ago, the business of making, selling, and buying things for our pets started to get underway. People were beginning to import fancy dogs from other countries, and the fashion for purebred dogs was gathering steam. In the 1880s, people opened stores to sell both pets—and things that storekeepers claimed that those pets needed. Owners felt that nothing was too good for their dogs, and pet stores were happy to help satisfy that feeling.

These new stores were designed to be attractive to

children and to ladies looking for an adorable furry or feathery creature to take home and love—and they came with a guarantee. Your pet-store canary would sing and your pet-store dog (a purebred one, no doubt, with behavior that was supposed to be predictable) would guard. If either the canary or the dog failed to do what was expected, you could bring them back and trade them in for a better one.

Pet stores didn't just sell pets and pet products. They sold ideas about what pets are for. And they created, and sold, ideas about what pets need and what their owners should do.

Collars, beds, toys, clothes, and food—all the things that we buy for our dogs today were also sold to owners in the earliest years of the 1900s. If we look at these things one by one, we'll start to see how we got to where we are today.

Collars

Collars are the first thing most people think of when it comes to buying stuff for a dog. As soon as we get a dog, we get her a collar.

As I look up from my desk, a photo of Pumpernickel, my longtime companion before Finn and Upton, catches my eye. She lies with her elbows sprawled, panting toward the camera with a half smile. I can nearly feel the softness of the fur around her velveteen ears.

One thing doesn't seem right: her red corduroy collar, a flurry of tags hanging off it. The collar, only a bit of cloth and metal, endures after her death: I finger it from time to time, and bring it to my face to remind me of her smell.

It bothers me that her collar now takes the place of the grace that was Pump. I never loved putting a collar on her—a flagrant sign of legal ownership, which felt at odds with her being my family. Still, the idea of putting a collar on a dog goes back thousands of years.

The oldest images of dogs we have yet found are sandstone carvings from eight thousand years ago. Other carvings on walls from five thousand years ago show dogs as well. In both, you can see that the dogs wear rope and metal collars. About twenty-five hundred years ago, many people and animals who died in Egypt were mummified, wrapped in cloth to be buried. This practice included dogs. If you look closely at one of the dog mummies, you can see a small tag on a collar poking out among the linen wrappings. About five hundred years later, a volcano erupted near the town of Pompeii, in Italy. The city and its people were covered in ash, and the ash mummified their bodies, which can still be seen today. Not only humans died in this tragedy; their dogs died as well. And from the casts made from their remains, we can see that they wore thick leather collars around their necks.

Those collars meant the same thing that a collar does today: This dog has an owner. One thing ownership means is control, after all. And a collar is a way to control a dog, to make her go where you want her to go or stay when you want her to stay. But collars are not only about making dogs do what people want. If that were all, collars would not be fancy. And yet they often are, and always have been.

Collars have been decorated and even covered in jewels for as long as they've been around dogs' necks. Dog collars have been discovered from ancient Egypt that are covered with gold and carved with a name. One dog's collar tells us that she was "Ta-ennût," or "She of the Town." Another ancient collar was made of white leather, decorated with pink and green insets and carved with images of horses. Others were studded with spikes or nails that would protect the dog from bites to the neck by another dog or a wild animal. In the sixteenth century, the Holy Roman Emperor Charles V had dogs who wore collars of velvet, leather, and silver. Collars like these said that the dog was *valued* as well as owned.

By the early 1900s, if you lived in America, you could get your dog any type of collar you could imagine—and a leash, lead, or muzzle as well. You want a spiked collar? Can do. Flat lined collar with a bell? Gotcha. Flat studded collar? Round with no studs? Round slip collar for training? Heavily studded round? Double harness leather spike bull collar for Boston, English, and French bulldogs? Fancy square studded? Jeweled? Glow in the dark? French calf leather round, decorated with studs and described in an ad as "an exquisite collar, fit for choicest animals"? Pet stores had you covered.

Owners might want something to hang on the collar as well. There were round bells and field bells, which "attach to collars of hunting dogs so that you may know their location . . . also quite the fad for use on street dogs," says the ad. Stores sold whistles and also "bangles," similar to dog tags today.

As people became more and more interested in purebred dogs, stores creatively began selling different collars for different kinds of dogs—to try to sell more collars. "A dog's collar should be suited to his breed," an early catalog insisted. "Long-haired dogs should have round collars . . . short-haired dogs look better in flat collars." Pomeranians and toy poodles were expected to have dainty collars. Bulldogs "needed" sporty collars. Choke collars were supposed to solve any behavior problem, from stubbornness to wildness to fearfulness. Whips and muzzles were sold as well.

Today's collars remain the same. We can buy collars that are decorations, in silk, nylon, chain, rope, and leather (with pearl studs or not, as we choose). We can buy collars that are supposed to control a dog or stop behaviors that we don't like—pulling, running away, jumping up (even though these behaviors can't be "controlled" by a collar).

All these collars say that the dog who wears them is with a person. A dog without any collar looks less like the true dog she is than like a lost one.

Dog Furniture

A dog is domesticated—a word that simply means "belonging to the house." And dogs not only live in our houses with us. They also sometimes have their own houses.

From the late 1800s and early 1900s, catalogs sold dog-houses. Kennels and shelters for dogs had been around before that, simple box-shaped structures to keep dogs out of cold or rain. By the 1920s, things had advanced. An owner could buy "the perfect dog house," or at least that's what the catalog claimed. This house had a slanted roof, a side door, and a protected entrance hall. It was "a cozy, dry, comfortable, scientific dog house . . . the house a dog would buy for himself." It cost thirty-five dollars—about five hundred dollars in today's money. Presumably most dogs could not afford it.

Dog not only have their own houses; they also have their own beds. Of course, most dogs would rather sleep in their human's beds, and some get to. King Henry IV of England allowed his greyhound, Math, into his bed. Not all kings followed his lead. King Henry VIII banned dogs from his court entirely.

At first, pet stores and catalogs sold straw or wood chips to line the floor of the doghouse, giving dogs a soft(ish) place to sleep. Over time, cedar shavings became the first choice, since they were helpful for keeping away bugs and bad odors. As more and more dogs were invited into their owners' houses to sleep, straw and bits of wood were replaced by the dog bed.

Some dog beds had mattresses with springs. Baskets with cushions (maybe hooded ones to keep off drafts) worked for small dogs; larger ones had comfortable chaise lounge chairs. One bed from Abercrombie & Fitch mimicked a bunk bed. It had a cushioned chair below for day use and a bed above for the night. By the 1940s, owners could have a dog's name embroidered on a blanket or a pillow.

Dogs had been invited inside the house for good, and they had their own furniture to prove it. In fact, soon, an entirely new product appeared on the market. These were

sprays (one was called Pup Pruf) that owners could use on chairs or beds to keep dogs off. Dogs had their beds, and humans had theirs—the only trick now was to get the dogs to stay in their own beds and off the ones that the humans wanted to keep for themselves.

Clothing

In the 1920s, ads for clothing were everywhere. Magazines like *Vogue* were chock-full of ads for coats, furs, frocks, gowns, riding habits, hats, and underthings for the fashionable lady. In 1922, a cover for *Vogue* showed a woman lazily patting her greyhound. The dog's thick jeweled collar matches the sash around the woman's waist.

Dogs didn't just help to advertise women's clothing; they were also supposed to wear their own. Greyhounds could wear everything from turtleneck dog sweaters "made of very fine worsted yarns" to waterproof raincoats. Dogs blankets came in plaid, leather, silk, and linen. The Abercrombie & Fitch catalog promised that their tweedy ulster coat was "made from the same fine imported tweeds used in our men's sports jackets." Dogs' feet were not neglected either. Owners could buy their dogs boots of calfskin leather or waterproof rubber. They even got eyewear: dogs who traveled in convertibles could wear goggles to keep their eyes from getting sore.

Underneath all these clothes, dogs' fur was taken care of too. By the early 1900s, pet stores offered to groom and bathe dogs for a fee. High Ball pet shop in Syracuse, New York, sold a "complete service for pets," which included clipping, shampooing, and manicuring. Abercrombie & Fitch advertised a Plucking & Grooming Service at their store in Manhattan. "Antiseptic bathing, nail clipping, tooth scraping and trimming are done on the premises," they promised.

Toys

Dog toys were one of the last products to be offered. A dog might sleep in a dog bed, wear a fancy tweed coat, and be groomed and trimmed and clipped in a pet store, but play with an old ball or a bit of string.

However, this state of affairs did not last long. As dogs began to be bred and bought and sold less to do a job (like guarding the house or herding the sheep) and more as friends and companions, the idea of needing to keep dogs amused began to take hold.

Pet-supply catalogs of the time tended to have a page or two in the back for the classic dog toys that are still popular today: balls, tugs, and chews. Some dog toys were more likely to be interesting or appealing to the owner than the dog, like the balls, bones, and rings that smelled like chocolate (actually toxic to dogs!), sold in the 1920s. Christmas stockings for dogs (then and now) are fun for humans, but a dog isn't likely to care if a treat or a toy comes inside a big sock or not.

Alongside the toys that were mostly for the owners came toys that a dog might reasonably be interested in. There were rubber toys or ones covered with fur, shaped like prey a dog might want to chase: a rabbit, a mouse, a rat, a cat. Many of these toys made crying or mewing sounds when shaken or squeaking sounds when bitten. There were also, oddly, rubber toys shaped like dogs' heads, with whistles inside to squeal when the head was gnawed.

Even with all these choices for toys, the idea of playing with a dog just for fun was new enough, it seemed, that it needed to be explained. Abercrombie & Fitch's tug toy came with directions: "You hold one end, dog pulls at other. Exercise for both master and dog," the catalog instructed.

Other Stuff

Pet stores and catalogs sold some extra things, too: products for dogs that were not clothes or furniture or toys. There are some we would not recognize today. Catalogs offered "tooth forceps" to pull out a puppy's first set of teeth. A "bulldog-spreader" was a harness that strapped over a bulldog's shoulders, meant to force the dog's legs wider apart.

A "tail shield" was a kind of collar or cone to be set on a dog's hindquarters, and it was supposed to protect the tails of Great Danes and other dogs from being hurt against the sides of their kennels. Some catalogs offered an "auto-stop" or a "stop chase," which was a contraption made of two heavy rubber balls that hung from a dog's collar. If a dog tried to run (perhaps to chase a car or a chicken), the balls would drag behind, slowing him down, or would thump against his side or tangle in his feet.

The fact that products like this aren't for sale anymore shows some positive changes in the way we care for our dogs. Owners today aren't likely to pull a dog's teeth out themselves, since most dogs see vets for this kind of thing, if it's considered necessary at all.

Perhaps Great Danes spend less time in kennels today than they used to, and we're more likely to keep our dogs on leashes or in yards than to leave them free to chase chickens and cars. And we may breed bulldogs to have wide chests and a waddling walk, but we don't force their legs sideways anymore, I'm glad to say.

The Invention of Kibble

This morning you fed your dog. Maybe you filled your dog's bowl with a pile of dry kibble or wet food from a can—or a chunk of raw meat with vegetables to go with it. Maybe your dog gets a few table scraps too, but most of what dogs eat is labeled "dog food."

As wolves were being domesticated, slowly turning into dogs, they scavenged from our food, eating what we didn't want. Dogs in the Middle Ages—the ones lucky enough to have owners—got a diet that was mostly bread. If the dog was too skinny, the bread was buttered.

So where did the idea that dogs need special food, eaten from special bowls, come from?

It began in the 1800s, when people began to sell food intended for domestic animals of all sorts. One ad from 1810 announced the sale of "good sound biscuit for dogs and hogs." These biscuits were hard crackers made of wheat, oats, or corn. They had to be soaked in "pot liquor"—the broth left after vegetables were boiled—before a dog (or a pig) would eat them.

In 1860, an American businessman named James Spratt noticed dogs hanging around a shipyard and gobbling up hardtack, a tough, bland biscuit made for sailors. Hardtack could last a long time on a voyage without rotting or going moldy. Spratt decided to sell something very much like hardtack as food for dogs.

Spratt didn't just make one kind of dog food. He created a variety: Greyhound Cakes, Oatmeal Cakes, Patent Cod Liver Oil Old Dog Cakes, and Pepsinated Puppy Meal. He used beetroot (a vegetable most people didn't know about) and "charcoal ovals" to create his products, and he sold them with "a guide to the choice of the correct biscuit for every known breed." Owners could buy Spratt's biscuits to feed aging dogs, puppies, city dogs, hunting dogs, toy dogs, and large dogs. And of course, no matter what kind of biscuits they chose, it made money for Spratt.

Dogs had existed very well on human scraps for centuries. They didn't really need biscuits made of beets, any more than they needed goggles or purses or heavy rubber balls hanging from their collars. But that didn't stop businesses from making dog food, or owners from buying it. Spratt's biscuits soon had to compete with many other dog-food makers, including Old Grist Mill, Pard, Miller's A-1 Ration, Dr. Olding, Old Trusty All Terrier, and Molassine.

It took longer for dog treats to come into existence. But by the 1930s owners could buy Chapen's dog cookies, Bow-Wow Bon Bons, and various dog "crackers." Maltoid Milk-Bones, shaped like a child's drawing of a bone, were first sold as meals. Only much later did they become treats.

The new food reflected a change in our attitudes toward dogs. People were thinking of dogs more and more as friends and companions, and also as show dogs admired for their looks. So business owners like Spratt saw a chance to convince dog owners that their special friends needed special food.

Some foods claimed to produce dogs who would win top awards at dog shows. Molassine boasted that its food "contain[s] Special Exclusive Features 'Patented' to produce Superior 'Condition' such as at once ASTONISHES THE JUDGES and secures the Highest Awards." Others claimed that their food would make dogs more healthy. Fish Biscuits prevented "Mange, Excema, Distemper," it claimed. Maltoid Milk-Bones said that they could improve the dog's coat, keep their teeth healthy, and build muscles. There was very little evidence for any of these claims, but that didn't stop ads from making them, or people from believing them.

Dogs who were stars in movies, TV and radio appeared in ads for dog food. Ken-L-Ration (along with Pup-E-Crumbles and Rib-L-Biscuit) boasted of being the favorite food of Rin-Tin-Tin, the German shepherd who starred in silent movies. Another TV and radio star, Lassie, a collie, plugged Red Heart 3-flavor dog food.

Dog food was also billed as convenient: quick to make and feed to a dog. When canned food for humans became popular, canned food for dogs was not far behind. Dog-food companies also claimed that feeding dogs table scraps could cause all sorts of problems—everything from over-weight dogs to finicky eaters. Best and easiest, they insisted, to feed your dog biscuits or canned food instead.

Businesses not only sold dog food; they sold the bowls to put it in. Most of these bowls look much like the dog bowls of today—except for one, my favorite. The "Spaniel Dish" had a narrow opening at the top to keep the dog's long ears from falling into their food. This might be the most useful object in all of the catalogs that I've seen.

What exactly went into these bowls—and into the dogs? The food might be made of wheat, oats, vegetables, ground bones, and some kind of meat—often horsemeat. (Horsemeat is no longer used in most dog food today.) Along with the food made specially for dogs came detailed instructions on how to feed a dog—something people never seemed to wonder about until dog-food companies started to tell them. These instructions told dog owners how many meals to offer their pets (usually two or three a day, sometimes six) and how much food to give the dog at each one. "Unfortunately," a Spratt's pamphlet explained, "dogs are not always able to distinguish between what is good for them and what they like . . . It is entirely up to you—his master—to insure your dog's health and longevity by proper feeding."

Dog-food companies sold medicine as well as food. They offered constipation pills, tablets for "fits" and dysentery, powders to kill fleas and give pep, lotions for ear cankers or mange, compounds for itchy dogs, healing salves, and coat growers. There were tablets and salves for rheumatism, pain in the muscles or joints. There were tonics and powders for fleas and worms, along with breath-sweetening mouth-washes. Dog owners bought the food, the medicine, and the advice.

Pet food companies not only told owners how to feed their dogs; they explained how to train them. The idea of a dog being polite or well-mannered was invented here, in pamphlets that pretended to advise owners while actually trying to sell them something. The training they describe mostly involved flicking dogs in the face and pulling them by the tails if they did something wrong, setting mousetraps to keep a dog out of garbage bins and off chairs, or yanking a dog by a leash or cord to teach it to stay in the yard. Yikes.

ALEXANDRA HOROWITZ

Today most of these training ideas have been replaced by the gentler, more effective idea of positive reinforcement—usually, feeding a dog a treat when he does what an owner wants. These treats are sold by dog-food companies, just as they were a century ago. In fact, most of our ideas of what to do with our dogs—what to feed them, how to train them, how to amuse them—are based on what dog-food companies and pet-supply catalogs began to tell owners in the early 1900s.

All of these products, from dog goggles to a Spaniel Bowl to a purse for your dog's collar, share one thing in common. They are made, sold, and bought because people care about their dogs. When dog owners wonder how they can show their dogs their love, pet stores and pet-food companies jump in to provide an answer. Whether it is the only way to show love is unasked and unanswered.

Now, as I look around the pet store, the Jack Russell terrier in the argyle sweater has left the building. I spy the round toys with the stumpy feet that Upton likes to chew off. I grab two. Then two of the blue-and-orange balls with the squeaker inside, for Finnegan. There's a box of those peanut-butter treats shaped like small gingerbread people, and some tough chews that look satisfying. I pick out some booties, since the dogs' feet have been getting stung on the salt put down on city streets to melt the ice. I give the cashier $64.76 and walk home to surprise my boys.

CHAPTER 10

THE DOG IN THE MIRROR

👣 👣 👣 👣 👣 👣 👣 👣 👣 👣 👣 👣 👣 👣

Over the years I've gotten a lot of questions from people who live with dogs about what, exactly, their dogs are doing. *Why does my dog . . . (fill in the blank: roll in things, turn circles, bark that way, lick that thing, sniff me, pee there . . .)*, they ask. But most of all we wonder: *What does my dog think about me?*

To answer this, we have to consider not just how dogs think, but also how people think about dogs. If we do this, it might teach us some things about ourselves.

Our Dogs, Ourselves

When we look at our dogs, we sometimes see in them what we would like to see in ourselves. We think loyalty is a good thing, so we believe that dogs are loyal. We want to believe that others are happy to see us, so we're pleased when our dogs greet us enthusiastically. We wonder what our choice of a dog reveals about us. Is the owner of a purebred poodle different, deep down, from the owner of a mixed breed?

In some ways we do seem to reflect our dogs. For instance, we look like them. People can match up a picture of an owner with a picture of that person's dog surprisingly successfully. Several studies have shown that if people are shown pictures of purebred dogs, they can match dog with owner more frequently than if they were just guessing randomly.

It's not that the dogs look like their owners, exactly— the guessers are not matching up a square-jawed man with a bulldog or a woman with frizzy hair with a poodle. Still, something is shared between person and pet. In one of the studies, one of the participants noticed that there was a picture of an owner with a goofy smile and a golden retriever with the same smile on his face. He matched them up—correctly.

I don't know if anyone would match up a picture of me with Pumpernickel, the curly haired, sheep-shaped dog who shared so much of my life. Or with sleek, earnest-faced Finn, or the awkward but charming Upton.

But it's definitely true that there are certain dogs I am drawn to. Expressive eyebrows make my heart leap. I'm a sucker for a shaggy beard and a soft gaze. Some people think that short-nosed dogs look adorable, but I worry about their health. I love to meet enormous dogs—Great Danes or Saint Bernards—but I don't really want to own one. Or tiny ones who could fit in my palm either.

Scientists who study why people make the choices that they do would say there's a simple reason for the kinds of dogs I prefer. I probably like dogs who are at least a little bit like me.

Most of our choices have something to do with ourselves. We tend to prefer the letters of the alphabet that are found in our names. We usually like the numbers that make up our birthdays. If we have a choice about where we sit, we often sit next to people who look like we do. This probably is part of why we pick the dogs we do.

It's not that we choose dogs whose fur matches our hair. But our dog's personality is often a match for ours. Anxious people are likely to have anxious dogs; outgoing people tend to have friendly dogs. We pick our dogs because something about them reminds us of ourselves.

We like person-looking dogs. In particular, we like dogs who have light-colored irises (like humans) and whose mouths form into a kind of smile (like humans' do). It's been suggested that we prefer animals whose features remind us of babies—anything with big eyes, a wide brow, and a large head is likely to get a reaction of, "Ooooh, so cute!" Similarly, dog breeds who have large eyes and overly big heads for their bodies are popular choices. Other animals with these traits are popular too—baby harp seals, say, or pandas. People linger near them in zoos and are willing to try to save them if they are endangered. They're less interested in saving the furless naked mole rat or a fleshy-nosed mandrill.

Dogs are like us and do what we do. Dogs rest when we rest and jump up excitedly when we get up. If we look at something, they look at it too. It's one of the things we love about them.

The first lesson that dogs teach us about ourselves is this: We like things that are familiar. When we have a choice, we choose animals who remind us of us.

Dogs as Dogs

If we look at dogs and see them as human beings covered in fur—well, that's not right, but it isn't all bad. That feeling of similarity helps us connect with dogs and care for them. It can be the first reason we love them. But it can cause problems as well.

If we expect our dogs to act like furry humans, we may not understand them well. We might think, for example, that a cringing dog with her ears tucked back is ashamed of herself. We might think she knows that it was wrong to tip over the garbage can. But that dog is actually reacting to an angry owner. She's trying to express with her body language that she knows her owner is the boss and has no intention of challenging him. The truth is, she actually doesn't understand a thing about the garbage except that it tastes good.

And there's a second problem that arises if we like dogs only because they seem sort of like humans. Sometimes it can be embarrassing and frustrating when the dogs don't *act* like humans.

And of course they don't.

They are dogs. They eat poo. They roll in poo. They stick their noses where you wish they wouldn't, chase what they shouldn't, and refuse to come when you call them. They sometimes pee in the house, they may pee in the elevator, and they might just pee on that person picnicking on the lawn.

We call it misbehavior. We get angry and even frightened of a dog who acts like an animal. If lightning strikes, we don't get angry at the lightning. We go indoors. We get out of the storm. If something natural is dangerous, we treat it with caution, but we don't hate it. But suppose a beloved pet is startled and snaps at a person? Then we *do* get angry. Often a dog who bites is euthanized with no attempt to figure out what caused the dog to react like that and what might prevent it in the future.

In the United States, there are about ninety million dogs living with people. And here is a sad but true fact about those dogs: They kill about twenty people a year. Each of these cases is a tragedy. But it is also extremely rare. In fact, your risk of dying by falling out of bed is about twenty-five times greater than your risk of being killed by a dog.

We don't get angry at beds. And we should probably not get angry at dogs, either. We certainly don't have to be frightened of them. We should, however, work harder to understand them. Then we might know how to treat dogs in order to keep them from biting. Maybe we should always try to keep in mind that dogs might remind us of people, but they are not *actually* people. A human would understand that you only want a hug, but a dog might panic at being suddenly grabbed and squeezed. A human would understand that you want to get rid of a damp, smelly bone on the carpet, but a dog might see you stealing her magnificent meal.

Dogs are animals—beautiful, impressive animals who are willing to live with us, to take food from our hands, to sleep on our beds (if they can get away with it). We will never understand them perfectly. That doesn't mean that we can't love them.

Maybe we shouldn't expect dogs to act just like humans. Instead, we can look at dogs and ask ourselves this: What kind of human beings are we? Do we understand the ways that dogs and other animals are different from us? Knowing that, can we still love them? Can we still take care of them? Can we look beyond dogs and take care of a world full of living things that are not exactly like us?

Dogs can help us do this, if we let them. They will help us by teaching us to value them and love them for the animals they are.

CHAPTER 11

HOROWITZ DOG COGNITION LAB BY THE NUMBERS

🐾 🐾 🐾 🐾 🐾 🐾 🐾 🐾 🐾 🐾 🐾 🐾 🐾

In the Horowitz Dog Cognition Lab, we study how pet dogs think and what dogs do. We collect a lot of information about dogs and also about people. Here are some of our statistics:

Year the Dog Cognition Lab was founded: 2008
Number of studies run since then: 11
Student researchers involved with the lab: 40
Number of owners who have called me "Dr. Dog" to my face: 2
Number of white lab coats kept at lab: 3

Who's Who

Number of live dogs kept at the dog lab: 0

Number of life-sized plush dogs kept at the dog lab: 2

Number of life-size plush dogs given names by experimenters: 2

Number of dog subjects: 531

Tail-waggers: 530

Tail-between-the-leggers: 1

Six most popular names, across studies: Charlie, Daisy, Lucy, Oliver, Oscar, Penny

Average number of legs of dogs in most recent study: 3.97

Blind dogs: 2

Deaf dogs: 1

Smallest dog: 7 lbs.

Largest dog: 155 lbs.

Experimental Details

Dogs injured during experiments: 0

Dogs poked with a needle during experiments: 0

Number of studies in which dog is tricked on purpose: 0

Number of studies in which owner is tricked on purpose: 1

Percentage of studies using hot dogs, freeze-dried liver or salmon, or cheese cubes: 100

Number of choir practices interrupted by dog barking: 1

Number of months an average study runs: 14

Highest number of hot dogs used in a single study: 34
Number of times experimenter says "Hi, puppy!
What's this, puppy?" in one study: 144

Dog Behavior

Average number of times a dog pees in the lab over
the course of a study: 2
Number of dogs who showed fear at a floor fan
with balloons on it: 15
Number of dogs who happily popped balloons: 1
Average length of time dogs sniffed canisters
containing a new odor: 3.3 seconds
Time one dog spent sniffing the canister: 120
seconds
Percentage of dogs who would still eat a hot dog
when it had been sprayed with lavender, mint, or
vinegar: 36
Number of dogs (out of 14) who immediately ate a
forbidden treat when their owner left the room: 1

Owner Behavior

Ten most common words owners say to their dogs
in a dog-human play study: you; good; it; get/
getting; got/gotta; go/going/gonna; come/c'mon;
(dog's name); girl; yay
Percentage of people who preferred dogs with large
eyes over dogs with small eyes: 59

Percentage of owners willing to submit their smelly T-shirts for a study of dog recognition of human odor: 100

Experimental Equipment Details

Video cameras destroyed by dogs during studies: 4
Number of times dog-shaped robot used in study attacked by dogs: 2
Rolls of sticky tape available to remove dog hair from clothing and chairs: 7
Number of toys dogs get to choose from as reward at end of study: 25
Number of dog toys dogs usually pick: 1
Number of dog toys one subject picked: 11

ALEXANDRA HOROWITZ

Bites, Pee, and Poo

Bites suffered by experimenter during studies: 0

Poo "accidents": 0 (we don't call them accidents: we're pretty sure they were all on purpose)

Number of studies involving owners collecting their dog's urine: 2

Number of pee cups ordered over two years: 220

Number of studies involving dog drool collection: 1

Number of studies involving human drool collection: 1

Amount of dog saliva on plush dogs at end of study: immeasurable

CHAPTER 12

DOES MY DOG LOVE ME?

🐾 🐾 🐾 🐾 🐾 🐾 🐾 🐾 🐾 🐾 🐾 🐾 🐾 🐾 🐾

I watch my own dogs nearly all the time. Finnegan and Upton are great furry balls of emotions and expression. I see when they're excited for a walk, disappointed at being left home, or grumpy when our friendly cat wants to curl up next to them.

When Finnegan drags a particularly large stick out of the river, I can't help seeing him as proud. When the cat curls up on my lap and he gives me a sour look, I must assume he's jealous. When I caught him last week sneaking mouthfuls of the cat's food, he certainly looked guilty.

But was he really?

🐾 🐾 🐾 🐾 🐾 🐾 🐾 🐾 🐾 🐾 🐾 🐾 🐾 🐾 🐾

Every day watching dogs, I see emotion in them.

In the lab, I see dogs who are *curious* about a small dog-shaped robot that dances and plays a tune. I see dogs who are *surprised* when someone comes out from behind a door. Dogs may feel *anxious* when I open an umbrella, *disgusted* when they sniff something, or *delighted* when their owner stops listening to me and turns to pet them again.

Outside of the lab, in parks and on sidewalks, I see dogs showing *joy*, *interest*, *affection*, and *fear*.

That dogs have feelings is clear. Still, some of the questions I am asked most often are about dogs' emotions: "Does my dog really love me?" "Do dogs feel bored?" "Do dogs get angry?"

Many of these questions start with people wondering if dogs have emotions at all. But of course they do: Everything about evolution, biology, and their behavior proves it.

Emotions are useful things. They are quick, direct messages to the nerves and muscles. If you see a tiger, you don't want to have to spend time mulling it over. Hey, I caught a glimpse of orange and black. Is it actually a tiger? Yep, I think it's a tiger. I know that tigers are predators. Predators might eat me. This particular tiger is coming toward me. . . . Instead of all this, the emotions cut in. That's a tiger! Be afraid! Run!

In human brains, there are particular areas that are active when we feel, sigh, long for something, or experience despair. Dogs have those same areas in their brains as well.

Dogs can't speak up about their emotions with words, but the way their bodies, ears, eyes, and tails move all tell us what's going on inside the dog. We aren't always great at reading the dogs' body language, but there's definitely a language to read.

I have no doubt that dogs (and other mammals) experience feelings. But that doesn't mean that their feelings are exactly the same as yours or mine. To think that dogs must feel exactly what humans feel is to make a mistake as serious as imagining that dogs have no feelings at all.

To see how common this assumption is, look at the dogs in movies. When a dog on screen covers her face with her paw, we quickly assume she's embarrassed or nervous. (What she is actually doing, of course, is performing a trained trick for which she'll get a reward.) Some dogs in movies actually talk—as if they are no longer dogs at all, but just small furry humans. When we're watching such a movie, we stop paying any attention to what the dog's body language says about how the dog is actually feeling. Instead, we believe the words set down by a human writer and spoken by a human actor, while the dog's mouth is made to look as if it's moving—as if this could tell us anything about what it's truly like to be a dog.

How can we understand what real dogs—not movie or TV or Internet dogs—might actually be feeling, instead of what we think or imagine or hope that they are feeling?

As a scientist, I don't yet have a way to test what a dog is feeling. Instead, I can observe what a dog does. And we can all learn to observe dogs carefully and start to get a sense of what dogs are experiencing inside.

In the lab, I carefully observe a dog's behavior—rather than assume I know what a dog is doing and, thus, feeling. I might say something like: "The dog's head extends forward, leading the body by an extra half step; the ears are perked into their full height." Is this dog curious? It certainly looks like it. Or I might note down that "a dog jumps back, preparing the body for escape; a 'rurf' sound slips out." Out of the lab, I might say that this dog is surprised. In the lab, I'm more cautious. The reason for this is that there are lots of different ways of feeling that could lead a dog to that behavior. To start, we just see what they do, and then later try to figure out what it means.

As well as being careful to record what a dog does instead of what I think she feels, I'm also careful not to assume that I know *why* a dog is doing what she does. For example, if a dog curls up next to a human when that human is sad, it's easy to assume that the dog feels sad for her—that the dog feels empathy.

But it's hard to be sure that this is true. One way to make a good guess is to keep a record of when it happens. Does the dog spend more time with a human who seems sad than with a human who seems calm and at ease? If lots of dogs spend more time with sad humans, we might decide that the dogs truly feel concern. If dogs spend a lot of time with humans no matter how the humans are feeling, the dogs probably just like being next to humans. And if you happen to have cheese in your pockets, that dog is probably next to you because she likes cheese.

What about another feeling? What about jealousy?

This is a feeling that seems to start when you notice that someone else has something you'd like for yourself. Most dogs like treats, so it seems reasonable to think that they might feel jealous if another dog has a treat and they don't. One study shows that most dogs will stop performing a trick if they see another dog doing the same thing and getting a treat for it, while they get none. But is this jealousy, or just a reasonable refusal to work for nothing?

Our lab ran a study to see how dogs reacted to unfairness in the giving out of treats. Would a dog prefer to spend time with a person who gave him just a few treats, and another dog many more? Or would the dog prefer a person who gave the treats out fairly? It turns out that the dogs spent more time with the unfair person than the fair one. This study suggests that dogs might not be feeling something like jealousy or resentment. They might just be hoping that they'll be the ones to get a big handful of treats next time.

How about empathy, or understanding what someone else might be feeling? It turns out that dogs are more likely to come near a sobbing human than a human who's humming a tune. Do they feel sorry for the person who seems to be crying? Or are they just not very interested in humming? More study is needed here.

Another experiment shows that dogs can be trained to pull on a tray to give sausage or cheese to a different dog. This looks like empathy. The dog can understand that another dog would like a delicious treat and will go to some effort to get him that treat. It gets more complicated, though. It turns out that a dog will pull on a tray to give another dog a treat, but dogs will *not* pull the tray to give a treat to a human. Not even their owners. So perhaps your dog does feel empathy—but not for you.

At the moment, science has a long way to go in understanding exactly what emotions dogs and other animals might be feeling. But it shouldn't be hard to learn more, because dogs are telling us what they feel all the time.

Their tails, eyes, ears, and spines—their entire bodies, not to mention their voices—are giving us clues about what's happening inside them.

We've been led to believe that what a dog feels is simple. Tail up, happy. Tail down, sad. But what about the tail wagging horizontally? Or wagging low, as the dog is crouching with ears flattened? Or stiffly wagging with the ears forward? These tails are showing us emotions that are more complicated than happiness or sadness.

If we keep looking, we might start to figure it out.

Does your dog love you? Watch him, and you tell me.

ALEXANDRA HOROWITZ

CHAPTER 13

MAKING PUPPIES

🐾 🐾 🐾 🐾 🐾 🐾 🐾 🐾 🐾 🐾 🐾 🐾 🐾

We were in a large New York dog shelter. The air was full of barks and the smell of wet dogs. Cages were stacked on cages. Nearly every one was full.

We poked our fingers through the cage of an impossibly cute puppy who had already learned to bark. We smiled at two puppies from the same litter, curled around each other. We lingered by the cage of a sad-faced two-year-old who had been adopted from this shelter once before and then returned.

It would have been easy for me to fall in love with any of these dogs. But I was trying to be careful. I knew we might be living with the dog we were about to choose for many years. I wanted to pick wisely.

Then we stopped by Finnegan's cage.

🐾 🐾 🐾 🐾 🐾 🐾 🐾 🐾 🐾 🐾 🐾 🐾 🐾

Say you live in the city with a dog or two. You're walking your dog, and you meet . . .

. . . a few smiling golden retrievers,

. . . a smattering of small furry white dogs wearing handknitted sweaters,

. . . a brown-and-black mongrel, just the right size,

. . . a beagle with lovable brown eyes,

. . . a black-and-white medium dog with a spot on his back like a saddle,

. . . a black-and-white small dog with a spot over one eye,

. . . a Rottweiler with a collar of metal links,

. . . and a wiggling, whimpering pit bull mix who can't wait to greet you.

Both you and your dog are happy to meet so many dogs out for a walk, just like the two of you are. But there is a sad fact hiding behind all of these happy pairs of dogs and owners enjoying the sun.

For every dog you meet on your walk, eighteen others have been euthanized because no one was able to adopt them.

Whose fault is this? I'm afraid it's ours. People created dogs out of wolves, and when we did that, we made a creature who cannot exist without us. Even stray dogs need humans, live near humans, and usually survive on the food that humans throw away.

But we don't take care of all these dogs we have created. And when they have puppies, there are even more dogs who don't have shelter, food, or love.

Spay and Neuter

Because no one wants all those dogs to die, many people in the US today, and for the last few decades, have said there is a simple solution to this very serious problem. Everyone, they say, should spay or neuter their pets.

To spay a female dog or neuter a male dog means having those dogs undergo an operation so that they will never be able to have puppies. It's also called sterilization, and it seems like a good idea. If we make sure that most dogs cannot breed, there will be fewer unwanted dogs who might end up as strays. Two thirds of all states in the US have a law to make sure all dogs adopted from rescues or shelters must be spayed or neutered.

Notice that these laws apply to rescues or shelters, not to breeders. Purebred dogs from breeders do not have to be sterilized. They can still have puppies. But dogs adopted from shelters are most often mixed breeds or mutts. They are the ones who are spayed or neutered before their owners even meet then. They will not have puppies, no matter what. And their owners do not get to be part of that decision.

So purebred dogs (who have their own troubles, as we saw in Chapter Seven) are allowed to have puppies. Mixed breed dogs (who are likely to be healthier) are not. Not if they come from a shelter, the most common place they're adopted from. That doesn't seem quite right. And it's just the first thing that should cause us to take a closer look at spay-neuter laws.

Before the 1930s, surgery to make sure dogs could not have puppies was very rarely performed. By the

1970s, ASPCA organizations were beginning to urge all pet owners to have their dogs (and cats, too) spayed or neutered. People were concerned with how many stray dogs and cats were hanging around neighborhoods; they thought of strays as dirty and dangerous. It costs cities money to round up stray dogs and cats and to have to put so many animals to sleep, not to mention it was terribly sad. Spaying and neutering pets seemed like the perfect answer.

It was also supposed to be good for the animals themselves. It would make them better behaved, people claimed—particularly male dogs. They'd be less aggressive, less likely to bark or bite. It would stop them from roaming around at night. And it would make it less likely for them to get certain kinds of cancers and infections. The idea of spaying and neutering dogs was supposed to be beneficial for dogs. It was supposed to make things easier for their owners as well. But we should look at the evidence to see if it has turned out that way.

At first glance, it seems that spaying and neutering pets has done exactly what it was intended to do: cut down the population of stray dogs who end up at shelters and may be euthanized if no one can find homes for them. In 1970, it is estimated that twenty million animals (cats and dogs included) were euthanized at shelters. Today that number is down to between two and four million.

This seems like a triumph for the idea of sterilizing pets.

But the truth is, it's very hard to come up with accurate numbers. Not every shelter reports the number of animals it is forced to euthanized. So these estimates may not be entirely correct. And lots of other changes in how we own dogs have happened too. When I was a child, people let their dogs out to roam the neighborhoods at night. Few people do that anymore. Now dogs are microchipped so that if they are lost, you can find them at a shelter. Before, if a dog was lost, even if it wound up at a dog pound, the owners might never know. And if you look carefully, it turns out that the numbers of animals in shelters started dropping in the 1940s, 1950s, and 1960s, well before spay and neuter laws became common.

It's also worth considering what has happened in other places. European countries like Norway, Sweden, and Switzerland have no laws requiring dogs to be sterilized. Seven percent of Swedish dogs are spayed or neutered. (In the US it's over 80 percent.) And yet there are very few stray dogs in those European countries. Why?

When I asked that question of author and scientist Stephen Zawistowski, who works for the ASPCA, he told me, "Dog ownership in Europe is a different concept." He added, "If you own a GSD [German shepherd dog] there, you probably belong to the GSD club." They take ownership seriously, and keep track of their dogs. In Switzerland, the law is designed to protect animals. It requires that no animal has any unnecessary surgery, like spay-neuter—so the Swiss have had to find ways to make sure that they don't let their dogs have puppies if they can't raise them or home them themselves.

All of this is interesting: Spay and neuter laws may have helped the numbers of animals in shelters drop, but they're not the only solution.

Problems with Spay and Neuter

The claims that spaying or neutering pets is good for dogs' health and behavior need a closer look as well. It's important to note that spayed and neutered dogs are more likely to gain weight. Their muscles are weaker, which can lead to trouble with bones and joints. Sterilization can also affect the way bones grow and the way the brain recovers if it gets injured. Spaying or neutering a dog may indeed mean that it's less likely to get certain kinds of cancers—especially those of the reproductive organs that are taken out. But a scientist named Ben Hart is looking very closely at the data of dogs, and he says that it turns out that some breeds will be more likely to get other kinds of cancer. The problems seem to be worse for large, pure-bred dogs; smaller breeds and mixed breed dogs get off more lightly. For many breeds, the health problems caused by sterilization are worse when the surgery is performed on young puppies.

What about the idea that neutering male dogs will make them better behaved, calmer, and less aggressive?

Studies show that this can happen—but only to about one dog out of four. The other three dogs show no change to their behavior. Females dogs who have been spayed actually may be slightly *more* aggressive if the surgery took place before the age of one.

The more we look at the information about what spaying and neutering does to the health of our pets, the more complicated the story seems to be. But there is one point that is not complicated at all: Sterilization is surgery. And surgery always come with some risk. It's a small risk, to be sure, but it's there.

We're usually okay with the risks of surgery, for ourselves or our pets, because we figure that everyone will be healthier afterward. The risk, we figure, is worth it. But it's still important to remember that any surgery can have problems, and some do. In our family, one surgery did.

Beezelbub

By the time our son was five, he had spent years admiring, waiting for, and petting any cat he came across (as long as the cat was willing). The bodega cat, the pet-store cat. The bookstore cat, the library cat, the street cat. Friends' cats, shelter cats, a cat on a tractor. In a house of dogs, my son pined for a cat to join them.

I was reluctant to add a new animal to our family, but I told him that "if we ran across a cat who needed a home, we could take her in." Of course, the next week

I ran across a cat. A beautiful brown, brindly cat, skinny and long, barely out of kittenhood, prowling the streets of Bensonhurst, Brooklyn.

I was on a walk when this small sprig of a cat crossed my path. She paused as I approached her. From above her back her tail curved into a question mark. I greeted her, then kept walking. She followed me for blocks, darting under cars and along the sides of buildings, keeping close but not too close. Concerned that I might be leading her away from her home, I doubled back and ducked into a bodega to buy some milk and a makeshift bowl for her. She slipped under the hedges lining a funeral parlor just as a man walked out of the building.

"Is this your cat?" I asked.

"Yeah," he said. "No. She lives here. She's not my cat."

"Is she a stray?"

He nodded. "She lives around here," he said.

I held out the milk toward him. "Will you give this to her?"

He shrank back. "No way. I'm not going to feed her." As he walked away, he said, "Take her—if you can catch her."

The next day I asked a friend who lived nearby for help. She found the cat, skillfully lured her into a box, and by that evening we had a cat.

"Beezelbub Jehoshaphat!" my son called out. The name didn't quite suit her, as she was a sweetheart of a cat, but it did show the delight and pleasure we felt with new animal energy in the house. (And she was a jumper.) She was a willing playmate, pursuing every small item on the floor and kicking it down the hall. She would madly race around corners and up shelves and the library ladder. Dangling cords thrilled her. Within a few weeks she had taken to joining me in my office and depositing herself squarely on my hands on my computer keyboard.

The dogs were alert and excited about her presence, and she was cautious and very aware of theirs, but they were forming an easy friendship. As is always the case, we soon couldn't imagine not knowing her.

I took her to the vet for shots and a checkup, and he recommended spaying her. I thought I should probably do what he said. Certainly, I had no reason to believe that this vet or any vet would give me poor advice.

Still, I knew she would be an indoor cat, and in New York City, indoors is indoors. There is no back door to accidentally slip out of. The windows are screened and guarded when open. She would not be going out. Instead, she would be sleeping with my son, who adored her, playing with the dogs, and quietly making sure I could not type on the computer.

The vet was persistent. He called me over and over. He knew more about animal medicine than I did. So I decided to do what he advised. We brought in Beezelbub to be spayed, about a month after she entered our home.

My son gave her a casual wave in her carrier, and we assured him he'd see her that night after school.

He didn't. Instead, I got a call from the vet while at work. Beezelbub had died before the surgery had even started, when he had given her a shot of morphine to make sure she would feel no pain.

I sat outside on the sidewalk and bawled. I had scooped this cat up from her life, "rescuing" her, only to send her to her early death. And I would have to tell my son. She was gone.

The vet was sorry, of course. "It happens only about one percent of the time," he told me. Only later did I reflect on this. One percent means that her chances of dying were one in a hundred. One in a hundred, for a surgery that she didn't really need.

If I had realized this, there is no question that I would not have sent her there.

To Spay or Not to Spay

Does a story like Beezelbub's mean we should stop sterilizing and neutering all dogs (and cats as well)? If we did, the number of stray animals, and the number of animals left at shelters, would almost certainly rise. No one wants that.

But there are other ways to prevent unwanted puppies or kittens, and I think it's high time we look at those ways. Plus, it's important to keep in mind that sterilizing pets is not the only way to deal with the fact that too many animals do not have people to take care of them.

We could just take better care of dogs in the first place. There is more to being a responsible pet owner than spaying or neutering a pet. That's not where responsibility ends; if anything, that may be where it begins.

Pet owners need to do more than make sure their dogs can never have puppies. They need to understand before buying a pet exactly how much time and money that pet will take up. They need to study their dogs carefully, learning how the dog lets them know when she's hungry, tired, done playing, or getting nervous. And owners need to understand what will happen if they do decide to let their dog mate and have puppies. If those puppies come along, owners must take on the responsibility of finding them good homes.

Spaying or neutering a pet might still be the right choice for some owners. But it should *be* a choice. Today, when people adopt a dog from a shelter or a rescue, they don't get a say. The decision is taken out of their hands. The dog will arrive sterilized, no questions asked—but questions *should* be asked.

With more data, people can start to answer questions like whether the surgery makes sense for the particular breed they have; at what age should this particular dog be spayed or neutered; and whether the benefits of the surgery outweigh the risks for *that dog*. It's a funny idea, that dogs should undergo a surgery to solve the problem that humans created: the overpopulation of dogs in our country. Maybe we should fix our problem, instead of fixing dogs.

Then the question can go from, "How can we make sure there are no unwanted dogs in the world?" to "What is right for my dog? This dog? This one right here?"

Meeting Your Dog

When I stood outside Finnegan's cage in that New York shelter, I was excited. But I was also cautious.

We asked to meet Finn, and a volunteer removed him from his cage. We took him to a gated area with a fake tree in it, near the entrance to the shelter. And there we watched him. We watched him for hours.

How did this dog react to people? Did he jump or snarl at sudden noises? What did he do when he was tickled on the ear? When we touched him on the rump?

Finn took a nap. We filled out paperwork. And we watched him more. What did he chew on? What caught his attention? What made him bark? What raised his hackles? Who was he?

As we got to know this cheery but calm puppy, at least a dozen people came into the shelter. They chose a dog or a cat and they left with their new pet. I grew more and more astonished.

If all went well, the people leaving the shelter might be

together with the dog or cat in their arms for as long as seventeen years. There was a seven-year-old leaving with a roly-poly puppy. Her dog would probably be with her until she was in high school, maybe even college. A young couple might be middle-aged and still own the dog they were leaving with today. But they probably took more time picking out the right pair of jeans in the store than they did picking out the right pet.

Shelters are eager to get the (spayed and neutered) animals in their care adopted to a good home as quickly as possible. After all, there are bound to be more animals coming in soon. But what if people took the time, as much time as they needed, to figure out if a dog was right for them before adopting one? What if more shelters offered classes helping people understand how to train a dog—how to figure out what a dog needs—how to live with a dog?

Maybe we would know our own dogs better and would understand more clearly what is right for each one.

And maybe—just maybe—there would be fewer dogs coming into the shelter. That might happen not just because we'd made sure our dogs could never have puppies, but because there would be fewer unwanted dogs in the world.

That's a world I would like to live in.

CHAPTER 14

HUMORLESS

If I tried to list the things that Upton does, that only Upton could do, I wouldn't even know where to start. He lies on the bed, so perfectly positioned that I'm forced to curl up like a baby in one corner. He thumps his tail to greet me in a way no other dog can do. He trots in a lopsided fashion down the hall. He has a galumphy way of greeting the cat, curled up in her box. His lip snags on a left tooth when he's thinking hard. And that's only by eight a.m.

Upton isn't trying to be funny. But all of the things he does make me happy.

Is it me?

I don't find movies with talking dogs funny.

I've watched lots of movies starring dogs, and I always hope that I will see something in the dogs that is new, different, surprising to me. My entire job is learning about dogs—what they think and feel; what it is like to *be* a dog. But this kind of science is just beginning, and I know how much we do not yet know.

I hope movies about dogs might offer me a new way to think about dogs. I keep thinking that maybe movie makers can show me something that scientists don't see.

But it hasn't happened yet.

A dog in a movie or on TV can be a genius professor (Mr. Peabody in *The Adventures of Rocky and Bullwinkle*) or a lovable goofball (Scooby-Doo in *Scooby-Doo*) or a thoughtful and loyal partner (Gromit in *Wallace and Gromit*). Often they talk, and sometimes their mouths even move, as in *Beverly Hills Chihuahua* or *Marmaduke* or *Beethoven*. But the one thing they aren't is *real dogs*. They have human voices and human emotions and they tell humans stories. We pretend we're watching a movie about dogs, but we're really just watching ourselves.

When it comes to dogs, I realized, I have become humorless.

I don't enjoy seeing YouTube videos of dogs in tuxedos or hats or pantyhose. I don't like GIFs of dogs forced to wear a crown of balloons.

Ever since I did a study to figure out if dogs with a guilty look are actually feeling shame, I haven't been able to find any humor in the sharing of "dog shaming" photos on the Internet. Dogs are pictured wearing signs announcing what the dog has done wrong. "I pooped on the rug," one might say. Or "Sorry I ate the lasagna off the counter." (Who left the dog in the kitchen with the lasagna? Shouldn't that person have a sign around his or her neck too?)

Many of these dogs have the classic "guilty look" I researched in my lab—tail tucked, back arched, head down. But my study proved that this look does not mean, "I know I did a bad thing." It is a submissive look, and it means the dog is aware that her owner is angry. If we put this look into words, it would be more like "Please don't hurt me" than "I'm sorry I did it."

Not very funny at all.

I don't like Halloween costumes for dogs. Nope, not even if you're dressing your dog up as Darth Vader or as one fourth of a Happy Meal. And by the way—making your dog sit there with a treat on her nose while you set up the camera isn't all that nice, either.

I'm surprised at how much I don't enjoy the things about dogs that other people think I'm supposed to find funny. Because I really, really like being with dogs. I feel reliable joy.

I'm always smiling around dogs. When I walk into a room with my dogs in it, I can feel my shoulders relax and my frown melt away. I laugh at my dogs' antics; I laugh with pleasure at how sweet or silly they can be. Seeing a dog walking toward me on a path is enough to make me smile.

There's a lot to laugh at in a life with dogs. But we don't have to humiliate dogs to find that laughter.

It's humiliating to pretend that dogs are something that they are not. Dogs are not Darth Vader. They are not natural wearers of tutus or hats. And they're not sorry they ate the lasagna. Actually, they enjoyed it very much.

Why pretend, when it is so much fun to watch what dogs do naturally?

Dogs are (probably) not embarrassed to be in costume. But it's not respectful to make them do something they only do because we want them to. Instead, what if we followed their lead? They're enthusiastic about the things they love. They don't hold back from what could bring them happiness. Living with dogs helps us be that way too.

I'm smiling now, thinking about this morning, when one of my dogs gently but firmly guided me to the door of every pet-food shop on our walk. I laugh when a dog greets me with crazy rump-wiggling fervor, licking my face all over. When have I felt that enthusiastic about meeting a friend?

As people, we tend to worry about how we look all the time. It's fun to be around dogs, who don't worry like this. They seem startled and fascinated by the air that bursts noisily and smellily out of their own rumps. They don't mind being caught on their backs with all feet in the air, drooling slightly, as they nap in the sun.

I'm gleeful at a dog who gets excited into zoomy running, frantic bursts of activity where the back legs sometimes get ahead of the front ones. I grin at the small dog who boldly or cautiously lifts her nose to greet a larger dog. I'm entertained by how much attention my own dogs pay to words that rhyme with "walk," "treat," "okay," and "cat." I'm amused by dog tails wagging together, at an older dog who patiently or grumpily puts up with a playful puppy, at dogs rolling in snow, searching, chasing, finding, retrieving, discovering, digging, gnawing things.

I find joy in dogs acting like dogs—in dogs being themselves.

When we dress our dogs up in costumes or mock them for doing something that comes naturally, it may feel like just a silly joke. No big deal. But it's one of the things that can keep us from appreciating who a dog really is.

The best way to interact with an animal, any animal, is to find a way to help them be themselves. Being cruel on purpose to a dog is wrong, of course. But not letting a dog experience everything that comes along with being a dog is also wrong.

What does a dog need? What should dog owners do to ensure that their dog is living a full life as a dog?

First, a dog needs a healthy body—enough food, clean water, medicine, and veterinary care.

Dogs need care for their minds and emotions as well. They need kind treatment, enough to do, and something or someone to love. When we give our dogs toys to play with and time with us and dog friends to race around with, we are fulfilling this need.

Dogs need more. They need a chance to move freely. They need to use all their senses, which means they need things to see, smell, taste, chew, touch, eat. They need a life that is full of experiences that are interesting and exciting for a dog.

They should have daily sights and sniffs, the chance to run around, to meet new things, to try something challenging. They also need to play, and not to play alone. They need not just time with you, but time on the floor with you, playing or wrestling or touching. They should be able to go outside, to smell the grass, to roll in dirt, to splash in water. They should be able to make choices: Hang out inside or go out? Play with the red ball or the rope toy? Curl up on the carpet or a pillow for a nap?

These are the things—the sniffing, licking, running, bonding, playing, choosing—that I already find joyful about dogs.

When I get up from my chair, Finnegan lifts his head, licks his nose, and slips off of the sofa to stretch his entire body. His eyes are alert to see what we're about to be doing together. He is entirely himself. He is completely dignified. And I am delighted to see him doing all of these things.

Is that funny? Yes! It's hilarious.

CHAPTER 15

THE TAIL OF THE DOG

🐾 🐾 🐾 🐾 🐾 🐾 🐾 🐾 🐾 🐾 🐾 🐾

My family's first dog was Gretel, an Airedale. I was barely speaking, so I didn't get to name her. When I was six, we met the softest brown-and-white springer spaniel puppy, Heidi, named by my mother after the Swiss girl of the story. For the rest of my childhood, I loved an Australian-shepherd-looking mutt named Aster—also by my mother—for his startlingly bright eyes, blue like the aster flower.

I don't know if I would've named him Aster. He was nothing like a flower: He was large, and liked to lie on one side in a lopsided fashion, sometimes entirely filling a lounge chair on our deck. His nose sustained many swipes from our annoyed cat, Barnabe, when he sniffed him too closely. He smelled like a dog, not like a flower. But after a few months there was no way his name could've been anything else.

🐾 🐾 🐾 🐾 🐾 🐾 🐾 🐾 🐾 🐾 🐾 🐾

e love our dogs. This is good news for them and for us, too. Each time a family adopts a dog, we show that we are willing to expand our circle to include them. We stretch our love and trust and our definition of family to draw in someone new.

We try our best to treat our dogs well. We scour pet stores for the best dog food, treats, and toys. We make sure they get walked, even if it means rushing home from school. We save a bit of dinner for them. We name them, talk to them, and get down on the floor to play with them.

On our worst days, we turn to our dogs and scratch their necks or let them lick us with affection.

Our dogs may not be human. Our laws may still treat them as things and possessions. But the way we treat them makes clear that our dogs are persons.

Even so, do we love dogs at all times? Something as simple as the words we use shows that we don't. The *doghouse* is the place you get sent to if you're bad. If you're *dog-tired* or *sick as a dog*, you aren't feeling your best. If you *hound* someone, you're nagging or pestering them. The *dog days* are hot and unpleasant. A *hangdog* expression is gloomy. *A dog's life* isn't one you want to live.

And what about the ways people treat dogs? We breed purebred dogs knowing that they may have short, painful lives. We leave dogs alone for hours and hours. Sometimes we even abandon or mistreat dogs. We love the ways our dogs are similar to us, but now and then we forget that dogs can't help acting like animals. Then we punish them just for being who and what they are.

Dogs aren't quite persons yet, at least according to the law. But they are ours. They cannot be anything else.

Dogs depend on us. They need us. Set a dog "free"— open up your door and let him go—and he will look for a way to connect with people again. (Don't do it!)

Dogs are our responsibility. We must take that responsibility seriously. So how should we treat these dogs we love?

First, we must take a hard look at them. We must figure out if some of our ideas about dogs are out-of-date or simply wrong. For right now, dogs are still property. We own them. But they are living property, animals under our own roofs. We can't treat them like chairs or tables. We also can't expect them to act like furry human beings.

The fact that dogs are animals is exactly what we love about them. How fabulous to have an animal in the house, an animal with her own mysterious thoughts and adventures! An animal who gazes at you, smiles at you, and listens with fascination as you tell her about your day. But we keep trying to get rid of the animalness of dogs. The way they smell. The fact that they need to pee and poop. The way they do unexpected things, animal things—growl over a tennis ball, poop in a corner, dig a hole in the lawn.

Animals have thoughts we can't guess; experiences we will never have; needs we can't imagine. They do things we cannot predict. What if we tried to accept dogs as the animals they are? What if we figured out how to enjoy and delight in the ways they are different from us?

Let's help dogs be dogs. Let's try to see them for who they are, so we can help them do what they are trying to do. Allow your dog to sniff that thing, to roll in that thing. Let dogs have your company. Find a way for them to do things they find interesting, to share time with humans and dogs whom they like.

We changed wolves to make dogs. Dogs change

us—humans as a species, and us as individuals—as well. They can make us wiser, kinder, more thoughtful. They can help us understand and love something and someone that does not look, act, or think just like us.

My dogs have changed me. I think about their feelings, their minds, about how to make their lives better. They've even changed what I see. Even after Pumpernickel died, I found myself walking close to certain trees with wide trunks because those were the kind she liked. On walks, I smile at signposts or corners of buildings—because they were things that *she* enjoyed. Finnegan has made me pay attention to giant rain puddles in the park. Because of Upton, I can't ignore garage doors crashing down or cars backfiring, since each of these sounds startles him. My time with my dogs makes a difference in the way I walk, the things I notice, and the habits that take me through my day. It has changed who I am.

How we treat our dogs shows who we are as people. Are we cruel? Are we lazy? Are we impatient? Or are we kind, thoughtful, and careful—even when no one but our dog is watching?

What kind of people would we become if we tried even harder to treat dogs as they'd like to be treated, and as they deserve to be treated? We'd be an animal I would be glad to know.

GLOSSARY

artificial selection: A human choice to allow only certain members of a species to mate and have young. Artificial selection is usually done to make a species or a breed more useful or attractive to humans. Also called selective breeding.

breed: A group of animals or plants that all have a similar appearance, different from other members of that species. Breeds are usually created by artificial selection, when humans choose which animals will mate and have young.

clone: A living thing whose genes are an exact copy of a single parent.

crossbreeding/crossbred: A human choice to allow members of two different breeds to mate and have young. A crossbred animal has parents of two different breeds.

domesticate: To change a species, through artificial selection, from wild (like wolves) to constitutionally tame (like dogs).

hypothesis: An educated guess, based on research or

observation, that can be tested by a carefully designed experiment.

inbreeding/inbred: When two closely related animals mate and have young. An inbred animal has two parents who are closely related.

purebreeding/purebred: A human choice to allow two members of the same breed to mate and have young. A purebred animal has two parents of the same breed.

selective breeding: A human choice to allow only certain members of a species to mate and have young. Selective breeding is usually done to make a species or a breed more useful or attractive to humans. Also called artificial selection.

NOTES AND SOURCES

Chapter 2: THE PERFECT NAME

8 *a beetle* Anelipsistus americanus:
All Latin name examples were found in John Wright's wonderful 2014 *The Naming of the Shrew: A Curious History of Latin Names.*

8 *indri, canary:*
Etymologies from the *Oxford English Dictionary.*

9 *"I had no idea that it would have been more appropriate . . . to assign each of the chimpanzees a number":*
Goodall, 1998, cited in E. S. Benson. 2016. Naming the ethological subject. *Science in Context*, 29, 107–128.

10 *And the truth is that scientists actually do name*:
Sharp, L. April 25, 2017. "The animal commons in experimental laboratory science." Talk delivered at the Human-Animal Studies University seminar, Columbia University.

10 *A human baby six months old can start to recognize his or her own name*:
Bortfeld, H., J. L. Morgan, R. M. Golinkoff, and

K. Rathbun. 2005. Mommy and me: Familiar names help launch babies into speech-stream segmentation. *Psychological Science*, 164, 298–304.

11 *names of expert hot-dog sniffers:*
Horowitz, A., J. Hecht, and A. Dedrick. 2013. Smelling more or less: Investigating the olfactory experience of the domestic dog. *Learning and Motivation*, 44, 207–217.

11 *Top dog names where I'm from:*
New York City Department of Health. "Dog names in New York City." http://a816-dohbesp.nyc.gov/IndicatorPublic/dognames/. Retrieved August 18, 2018.

12 *American Kennel Club naming rules:*
http://www.akc.org/register/naming-of-dog/. Retrieved August 8, 2017.

13 *"Spigot," "Bubbler," etc.:*
Xenophon. "On Hunting." http://bit.ly/2vT8hx3 & http://bit.ly/2womJOG.

13 *Alexander the Great named his dog:*
O'Brien, J. M. 1994. *Alexander the Great: The Invisible Enemy.*

13 *Recommended names for hunting dogs of the Middle Ages:*
Walker-Meikle, K. 2013. *Medieval Dogs.*

13 *A book on hunting hounds from 1706:*
October 6, 1888. *Notes and Queries.* http://bit.ly/2wlM-NXY.

13 *George Washington's dogs:*

Grier, K. 2006. *Pets in America: A History*, p. 34.

14 *Mark Twain's dogs:*

Zacks, R. 2016. *Chasing the Last Laugh: Mark Twain's Raucous and Redemptive Round-the-World Comedy Tour.*

14 *a man named Carl claimed "the name of Rock":*

August 19, 1876. *Chicago Field.*

14 *children's magazines from that time:*

1879–1880. *Harper's Young People*, 20 volumes.

15 *Hartsdale Pet Cemetery first pet:*

https://www.hartsdalepetcrematory.com/about-us/our-history/.

15 *Hartsdale gravestone names:*

Brandes, S. 2009. The meaning of American pet cemetery gravestones. *Ethnology*, 48, 99–118.

15 *a columnist for the New York Times asked readers to send in their dogs' names:*

December 22, 1985. "On Language: Name that dog." *New York Times* magazine.

Chapter 3: PET OR PROPERTY

25 *ownership of Willow and Kenya:*

2016. Henderson v. Henderson (Canada). https://www.canlii.org.

26 *Dogs are family:*

2015. The Harris Poll. https://theharrispoll.com/americans-have-always-had-interesting-relationships-with-their-pets-whether-that-pet-is-a-cat-dog-parakeet-

or-something-else-the-pet-industry-is-thriving-and-for-
good-reason-more-than-three-in-f/

27 *have dominion over the fish of the sea:*
Genesis 1:28, King James Version.

27 *later verses in the Bible:*
Proverbs 12:10 and Hosea 2:18, respectively, via K.
Thomas. 1996. *Man and the Natural World: Changing
Attitudes in England 1500–1800*, p. 24.

27 *Greek and Roman laws:*
Wise, S. M. 2003. The evolution of animal law since
1950. In D. J. Salem and A. N. Rowan, eds. *The State of the
Animals*, vol. II, pp. 99–105; also "The common law and
civil law traditions." School of Law, UC Berkeley.
https://www.law.berkeley.edu/wp-content/
uploads/2017/11/CommonLawCivilLawTraditions.pdf

27–28 *views of René Descartes and Immanuel Kant:*
Francione, G. L. 2004. Animals—Property or per-
sons? In C. R. Sunstein and M. C. Nussbaum, eds. *Animal
Rights: Current Debates and New Directions*, pp. 108–142.
Also see Kant, *Anthropology*, from a pragmatic point of
view.

29 *Charles Darwin, all living species are related:*
Darwin, C. (1871) 2004. *The Descent of Man*. London:
Penguin.

29 *Jeremy Bentham, animals can clearly suffer pain:*
Bentham, J. 1823. *An Introduction to the Principles of
Morals and Legislation*. Chapter XVII, section 1, para-
graph IV, and footnote 122.

32 *dogs as collateral:*
Francione 2004, pp. 116–117.
32 *animals used for research, product testing, etc.:*
Francione 2004, p. 109.
32 *a good number are dogs:*
United States Department of Agriculture. 2016.
Animal and Plant Health Inspection Service. *Annual Report Animal Usage by Fiscal Year.* In 2016 that number was 60,979.
33 *dog cloning:*
For more on this topic, see, e.g., Brogan, J. March 22, 2018. "The real reasons you shouldn't clone your dog." Smithsonian.com; Duncan, D. E. August 7, 2018. "Inside the very big, very controversial business of dog cloning." *Vanity Fair*; Hecht, J. March 6, 2018. "The hidden dogs of dog cloning." *Scientific American* blog.

Chapter 4: MORE THAN ONE TYPE OF PERSON

36 *keeping animals as pets is simply wrong:*
Francione, G. L., and A. E. Charlton. "The case against pets." Aeon. https://aeon.co/essays/why-keeping-a-pet-is-fundamentally-unethical.
38 *"Here is Plato's man!":*
Branham, R. B., and M.-O. Goulet-Cazé, eds. 2000. *The Cynics: The Cynic Movement in Antiquity and Its Legacy*, p. 88.
38 *the list of what makes humans different from other animals:*

I've written a little more about this here: "Are humans unique?" www.psychologytoday.com/us/blog/minds-animals/200907/are-humans-unique.

41 *a chimpanzee named Tommy is a person:*
Walsh, B. December 2, 2013. "Do chimps have human rights? This lawsuit says yes." *Time.* Also see https://www.nonhumanrights.org/blog/lawsuit-filed-today-on-behalf-of-chimpanzee-seeking-legal-personhood/.

41 *you do not have to be a human being to be a legal person:*
https://www.lawinsider.com/clause/person.

41 *a chimp in Argentina named Cecilia:*
"The first 20 days of Cecilia." http://www.projetogap.org.br/en/noticia/the-first-20-days-of-cecilia/. See also "Chimpanzee recognized as legal person." https://www.nonhumanrights.org/blog/nonhuman-rights-project-praises-argentine-courts-recognition-of-captive-chimpanzees-legal-personhood-and-rights/.

41 *Whanganui River in New Zealand; the Ganges and the Yamuna in India*
Roy, E. A. March 16, 2017. New Zealand river granted same legal rights as human being. TheGuardian.com; Safi, M. March 21, 2017. Ganges and Yamuna rivers granted same legal rights as human beings. TheGuardian.com.

43 *living property:*
Favre, D. 2000. Equitable self-ownership for animals. *Duke Law Journal*, 50, 473–502.

000 *consider the "well-being" of a dog:*

Alaska: Amendment to AS 25.24.160, Chapter 24 on Divorce and Dissolution of Marriage. See https://www.animallaw.info/statute/ak-divorce-% C2%A7-2524160-judgment; for Illinois see http://www. ilga.gov/legislation/ilcs/ilcs5.asp?ActID=2086.

46 *full dogness:*
This list inspired in part by M. C. Nussbaum. 2004. Beyond "compassion and humanity": Justice for nonhuman animals. In C. R. Sunstein and M. C. Nussbaum, eds. *Animal Rights: Current Debates and New Directions*, pp. 299–320.

Chapter 5: THINGS PEOPLE SAY TO THEIR DOGS

52 *"Coom, biddy":*
K. Thomas. 1996. *Man and the Natural World: Changing Attitudes in England 1500–1800*, pp. 95–97.

53 *"Well, well!" he says to the dog, Jip:*
Lofting, H. (1920) 1948. *The Story of Doctor Dolittle*, p. 150.

54 *a high-pitched, singsongy voice:*
Ben-Aderet, T., M. Gallego-Abenza, D. Reby, and N. Mathevon. 2017. Dog-directed speech: Why do we use it and do dogs pay attention to it? *Proceedings of the Royal Society B*, 284.

54 *They also repeat words:*
See, e.g., Jeannin, S., C. Gilbert, and G. Leboucher. 2017. Effect of interaction type on the characteristics

of pet-directed speech in female dog owners. *Animal Cognition*, 20, 499–509.

54 *an adult will often stretch out his or her vowel sounds:*
Burnham, D., C. Kitamura, and U. Vollmer-Conna. 2002. What's new, pussycat? On talking to babies and animals. *Science*, 296, 1435.

55 *Yurok Indians:*
Serpell, J. 2017. From paragon to pariah: Cross-cultural perspectives on attitudes to dogs. In his *The Domestic Dog: Its Evolution, Behavior, and Interactions with People*, p. 303.

59 *Gimme paw! Gimme paw!:*
Shared with me via Twitter.

62 *Forever Unanswered Questions:*
As noted by Beck and Katcher 1983 (in Arluke and Sanders 1996) in their observations of owner-veterinarian interactions.

63 *"Bye-bye, Max." "See you tomorrow, little guy."*
Robins, D. M., C. R. Sanders, and S. E. Cahill. 1991. Dogs and their people: Pet-facilitated interaction in a public setting. *Journal of Contemporary Ethnography*, 20, 3–25.

63 *dogs are all listening and no talking back:*
Fudge, E. 2008. *Pets (Art of Living)*, p. 52.

64 *"I hate to walk alone—":*
December 1827. *Blackwood's Edinburgh magazine*, pp. 731–733.

65 *"best slumber party ever":*
https://www.instagram.com/p/BPxjyQdADq9/?hl=
en&takenby=chloetheminifrenchie.

65 *Instagram dogs model clothes:*
Newman, A. July 13, 2017. "This Instagram dog wants
to sell you a lint roller." *New York Times.*

65 *Normally, people with power:*
Arluke, A., and C. R. Sanders. 1996. *Regarding Animals*,
p. 62.

65 *Of a dog lying down at the vet's:*
Arluke and Sanders 1996, p. 67.

66 *an effort to understand their point of view:*
Goffman 1981, in Tannen, D. 2007. Talking to the dog:
Framing pets as interactional resources in family discourse.
In D. Tannen, S. Kendall, and C. Gordon, eds. *Family Talk:
Discourse and Identity in Four American Families.*

67 *I love you:*
2002. "Did you know . . ." *Canadian Veterinary Journal*,
43, 344.

67 *Even the simple sound of our voice:*
Tannen also talks about talk as sound.

Chapter 6: THE TROUBLE WITH BREEDS

68 Clumber spaniel breed standard (Note: Breed standards can also be found on the American Kennel Club
website and are widely available online): The Clumber
Spaniel Club of America website: https://www. clumbers.

org/index.php/clumbers/breed-standard/official-akc-standard. Retrieved February 23, 2019.

69 *"Bunny-tailed Scottish Shepterrier" etc.:*
From Territorio de Zaguates.

70 *Sloughi breed standard:*
https://www.akc.org/dog-breeds/sloughi/. Retrieved February 23, 2019.

71 *over fifty million members over the years:*
Ghirlanda, S., A. Acerbi, H. Herzog, and J. A. Serpell. 2013. Fashion vs. function in cultural evolution: The case of dog breed popularity. *PLOS ONE*, 8, e74770.

72 *Medieval tapestries:*
Such as the Bayeux Tapestry, eleventh century; and Journey of the Magi, 1435.

72 *A painting of a wedding scene:*
Jan Van Eyck's Arnolfini portrait

72 *Nearly a hundred years later, another list described:*
Caius, Johannus. 1576. *De Canibus Britannicus*, translated as *Of Englishe dogges*. https://archive.org/details/ofenglishedogges00caiuuoft. See also Ritvo, H. 1989. *The Animal Estate: The English and Other Creatures in Victorian England*, pp. 93–94.

74 *Welsh springer spaniel breed standard:*
Welsh Springer Spaniel Club of America website: https://www.wssca.com/html/welshStandard.html. Retrieved February 23, 2019.

75 *Horand von Grafrath:*
Stephanitz, V. 1923. "The German Shepherd dog in

word and picture." http://bit.ly/2ypKweZ.

76 Newcastle-upon-Tyne show:

Pemberton, N., and M. Worboys. June 2009. "The surprising history of Victorian dog shows." *BBC History* magazine.

76 first winner at Newcastle:

Lane, C. H. 1902. *Dog Shows and Doggy People*; Sampson, J., and M. M. Binns. 2006. The Kennel Club and the early history of dog shows and breed clubs. In E. A. Ostrander, U. Giger, and K. Lindblad-Toh, eds. *The Dog and Its Genome*, pp. 19–30.

77 *the best bulldogs*:

Ritvo 1989, p. 112; see also Maj. J. M. Taylor. (1874–1891) 1892. Bench Show and Field Trial records and standards of dogs in America and valuable statistics.

77 *cocker spaniel, mastiff, English pug*:

spaniel and pug: Taylor 1892; mastiff breed standard 1887.

Grier 2006, p. 44.

79 *"Nobody now who is anybody"*:

Ritvo 1989, pp. 92–93.

Chapter 7: MORE TROUBLE WITH BREEDS

82 *German shorthaired pointer breed standard*:

German Shorthaired Pointer Club of America website: http://www.gspca.org/Breed/Standard/index.html. Retrieved February 23, 2019.

83 *results of inbreeding*:

Bateson, P. 2010. Independent inquiry into dog breeding; see also Asher, L., G. Diesel, J. F. Summers, P. D. McGreevy, L. M. Collins. 2009. Inherited defects in pedigree dogs. Part 1: Disorders related to breed standards. *The Veterinary Journal*, 182, 402–411.

83 *Those bulldogs from a century and a half ago:*

S. Zawistowski, phone interview, July 18, 2017.

84 *bulldog appearance:*

See Bateson 2010.

84 *People tend to find animals with flat faces adorable:*

Hecht, J., and A. Horowitz. 2015. Seeing dogs: Human preferences for dog physical attributes. *Anthrozoös*, 28, 153–163.

87 *Breeds do tend to react alike to certain things that catch their attention:*

See, e.g., Merkham, L. R., and C. D. L. Wynne. 2014. Behavioral differences among breeds of domestic dogs (Canis lupus familiaris): Current state of the science. *Applied Animal Behaviour Science*, 155, 12–27.

87 *Breeds that were developed to do a particular job:*

Hecht, J., and A. Horowitz. 2015. Introduction to dog behavior. In E. Weiss, H. Mohan-Gibbons, and S. Zawitowski, eds. *Animal Behavior for Shelter Veterinarians and Staff*, pp. 5–30.

88 *golden retriever breed standard:*

https://www.grca.org/about-the-breed/akc-breed-standard/.

88 *"good with children":*
http://www.akc.org/dog-breeds/golden-retriever/.
Retrieved October 8, 2017.

88 *One study compared the reports of aggressive behavior of golden retrievers:*
Ott, S. A., E. Schalke, A. M. von Gaertner, and H. Hackbarth. 2008. Is there a difference? Comparison of golden retrievers and dogs affected by breed-specific legislation regarding aggressive behavior. *Journal of Veterinary Behavior*, 3, 134–140.

89 *the Spitz:*
May 24, 1876. "A whited canine sepulchre." *New York Times.*

89 *"Terrorists on four legs":*
June 4, 1989. *The Observer* (London), p. 13.

89 *The UK law banned four breeds:*
Taylor and Signal 2011.

90 *banned dogs:*
See, e.g., https://petolog.com/articles/banned-dogs.html.

90 *President Teddy Roosevelt had a pit bull in the White House:*
Dickey, B. 2016. *Pit Bull: The Battle over an American Icon*, p. 13.

90 *what Teddy Roosevelt's bull terrier did:*
May 10, 1907. "Pete bites a visitor." *Washington Post*, p. 1; May 13, 1907. "President's dog licked." *The Tennessean*, p. 5; May 10, 1907. "Pete the bulldog gets a victim." *New*

York Times, p. 1; May 11, 1907. "Plebian pup beats White House Pete." *New York Times*, p. 5.

91 *history and confusion over pit bulls:*
Dickey 2016, pp. 157, 270.

91 *breed bans don't work to reduce dog attacks:*
Serpell 2017.

91 *One study looked at bans that affected thirteen different breeds of dogs:*
Forkman, B., and I. C. Meyer. 2018. The effect of the Danish dangerous dog act on the level of dog aggressiveness in Denmark. Paper presented at International Society of Applied Ethology meeting, Prince Edward Island, Canada.

92 *dachshunds:*
See, e.g., Duffy, D. L., Y. Hsu, and J. A. Serpell. 2008. Breed differences in canine aggression. *Applied Animal Behaviour Science*, 114, 441–460.

93 *puppy mills:*
ASCPA. "A closer look at puppy mills." https://www.aspca.org/animal-cruclty/puppy-mills/closer-look-puppy-mills-old.

93 *pet stores and puppy mills:*
See, e.g., https://www.aspca.org/animal-cruelty/puppy-mills; http://www.humanesociety.org/assets/facts-pet-stores-puppy-mills.pdf.

Chapter 9: DOG STUFF

107 *Canine Styles website:*
https://www.caninestyles.com/.

108 pawbag:
https://www.today.com/money/luxury-hand-bags-godogs-2D79703332.
108 dog cologne:
https://www.dogfashionspa.com/maschio-dog-cologne.
108 *dog nail polish and bathrobe*:
https://www.dogfashionspa.com/dog-nail-polish-dog-nail-file-dog-nail-care.
108 *nineteenth-century pet stores*:
Grier 2006, pp. 308–311.
108 *pet shops selling things for dogs' toys:*
As early as 1887: newspapers.com.
110 *earliest surviving imagery of dogs include collars and leashes:*
http://www.sciencemag.org/news/2017/11/these-may-be-worlds-first-images-dogs-and-theyre-wearing-leashes.
110 *other carvings on walls from five thousand years:*
Johns, C. 2008. *Dogs: History, Myth, Art.*
110 *ancient Egyptian mummified dogs:*
From 510 to 230 BCE. "Soulful creatures." Brooklyn Museum. 2018; https://www.brooklynmuseum.org/exhibitions/soulful_creatures_animal_mummies.
111 *Egyptian collars:*
Phillips, D. 1948. *Ancient Egyptian Animals*, p. 28.
111 *decorated collars:*
Pickeral, T. 2008. *The Dog: 5000 Years of the Dog in Art*, p. 30.

111 *spiked collars:*
Kalof 2007; Grier 2006.

112 *"A dog's collar should be suited to his breed":*
Q-W Dog Remedies and Supplies, 1922.

112 *choke collar:*
The Dog Breakers' Guide, vol. 2, no. 10, 1878.

113 *"the house a dog would buy for himself":*
Q-W Dog Remedies and Supplies, 1922, p. 46.

113 *Henry VIII:*
Walker-Meikle 2013, pp. 59, 64.

114 *bunk bed:*
Abercrombie & Fitch catalog, 1937.

115 *Vogue covers:*
Vogue 1915; January 15, 1922.

117 *"Exercise for both master and dog":*
Abercrombie & Fitch catalog, 1942.

117 *tooth forceps and tail shield:*
Abercrombie & Fitch catalog, 1937, p. 14.

117 *bulldog spreader:*
March 16, 1907. The American Stock Keeper (Boston).

117–118 *auto-stop, dog goggles:*
Q-W Dog Remedies and Supplies, 1922.

118 *Middle Ages dog diet:*
Walker-Meikle 2013, pp. 37, 44.

119 *"Good sound biscuit for dogs and hogs":*
October 18, 1819. *The Times* (London).

119 *biscuits had to be soaked:*
February 5, 1825. *Jackson's Oxford Journal.*

119 *James Spratt:*
Grier 2006, p. 367.

119 *other biscuit brands:*
See, e.g., March 16, 1907. *American Stock Keeper* (Boston), vol. 36, no. 11.

120 *dog-food diets:*
See, e.g., March 24, 1897, *New York Times*, p. 8; Dog biscuits—e.g., Champion Dog biscuits—made the same appeal. See, e.g., March 11, 1925, *Indiana* (PA) *Progress*.

120 *Maltoid Milk-Bones:*
November 15, 1910. *Hartford Courant*, p. 6.

000 *Rin-Tin-Tin's food:*
December 1, 1926. *Belvidere Daily Republican*, p. 5.

121 *Lassie's food:*
April 14, 1949. *Chicago Tribune*, part 3 p. 12.

122 *"dogs are not always able to distinguish between what is good for them":*
Spratt's pamphlet.

122 To teach a dog to stay in the yard:
"How to care for your new dog." Purina Dog Care pamphlet.

122 *dog politeness:*
Abercrombie & Fitch catalog, 1937.

Chapter 10: THE DOG IN THE MIRROR

125 *People can match up a picture of an owner with a picture of that person's dog:*
Roy, M. M., and N. J. S. Christenfeld. 2004. Do dogs

resemble their owners? *Psychological Science*, 15, 361–363; Roy, M. M., and N. J. S. Christenfeld. 2005. Dogs still do resemble their owners. *Psychological Science*, 16, 9; Nakajima, S., M. Yamamoto, and N. Yoshimoto. 2015. Dogs look like their owners: Replications with racially homogenous owner portraits. *Anthrozoös*, 22, 173–181; Payne, C., and K. Jaffe. 2005. Self seeks like: Many humans choose their dog pets following rules used for assortative mating. *Journal of Ethology*, 23, 15–18.

125 *an owner with a goofy smile and a golden retriever:* Bhattacharya, S. 2004. Dogs do resemble their owners, finds study. *New Scientist*.

126 *letters of our name and numbers of our birthday:* Jones, J. T., B. W. Pelham, M. C. Mirenberg, and J. J. Hetts. 2002. Name letter preferences are not merely mere exposure: Implicit egotism as self-regulation. *Journal of Experimental Social Psychology*, 38, 170–177.

126 *we often sit next to people who look like we do:* Mackinnon, S. P., C. H. Jordan, and A. E. Wilson. 2011. Birds of a feather sit together: Physical similarity predicts seating choice. *Personality and Social Psychology Bulletin*, 37, 879–892.

126 *Anxious people are likely to have anxious dogs:* Schöberl, I., M. Wedl, A. Beetz, K. Kotrschal. 2017. Psychobiological factors affecting cortisol variability in human-dog dyads. *PLOS ONE*, 12, e0170707.

126 *outgoing people tend to have friendly dogs:*

NOTES AND SOURCES

Turcsán, B., F. Range, Z. Virányi, A. Miklósi, and E. Kubinyi. 2012. Birds of a feather flock together? Perceived personality matching in owner-dog dyads. *Applied Animal Behaviour Science*, 140, 154–160.

127 *we prefer animals whose features remind us of babies:*
Lorenz, K. (1950) 1971. Ganzheit und Teil in der tierischen und menschlichen Gemeinschaft. Reprinted in R. Martin, ed., *Studies in Animal and Human Behaviour*, vol. 2, pp. 115–195.

127 *Other animals with these traits are popular too:*
Kellert, S. R. 1996. *The Value of Life: Biological Diversity and Human Society.*

127 *Dogs rest when we rest and jump up excitedly when we get up:*
Duranton, C., T. Bedossa, and F. Gaunet. 2017. Interspecific behavioural synchronization: Dogs present locomotor synchrony with humans. *Scientific Report*, 7, 12384.

129 *deaths due to dog attacks:*
See, e.g., Langley, R. L. 2009. Human fatalities resulting from dog attacks in the United States, 1979–2005. *Wilderness & Environmental Medicine*, 20, 19–25; The Center for Disease Control numbers for years since are commensurate.

129 *risk of death by falling out of bed:*
Per 2014 National Safety Council numbers indicating 38 dog-bite deaths and 1,045 bed-falling deaths. Johnson, R., and L. Gamio. November 17, 2014. "Ebola is the least of your worries." *Washington Post.*

Chapter 12: DOES MY DOG LOVE ME?

136 *the "guilty look":*
Horowitz, A. 2009. Disambiguating the "guilty look": Salient prompts to a familiar dog behavior. *Behavioural Processes*, 81, 447–452; Hecht, J., Á. Miklósi, M. Gácsi. 2012. Behavioural assessment and owner perceptions of behaviours associated with guilt in dogs. *Applied Animal Behaviour Science*, 139, 134–142.

140 *most dogs will stop performing a trick:*
Range, F., L. Horn, Z. Virányi, and L. Huber. 2008. The absence of reward induces inequity aversion in dogs. *Proceedings of the National Academy of Sciences of the United States of America*, 106, 340–345.

140 *how dogs reacted to unfairness in the giving out of treats:*
Horowitz, A. 2012. Fair is fine, but more is better: Limits to inequity aversion in the domestic dog. *Social Justice Research*, 25, 195–212.

141 *So perhaps your dog does feel empathy—but not for you:*
Quervel-Chaumette, M., G. Mainix, F. Range, S. Marshall-Pescini. 2016. Dogs do not show pro-social preferences towards humans. *Frontiers of Psychology*.

Chapter 13: MAKING PUPPIES

144 *For every dog you meet on your walk, eighteen others have been euthanized:*
As discussed later in the chapter, exact numbers about

how many dogs are euthanzied are hard to come by. This number is based on the figure of 670,000 dogs killed, from the ASPCA in 2017: https://www.aspca.org/animal-homelessness/shelter-intake-and-surrender/pet-statistics. Retrieved May 8, 2017.

144 *history of spay-neuter (and shelters):*
Grier 2006, pp. 102ff; Zawistowski, S. 2008. *Companion Animals in Society.*

146 *And it would make it less likely for them to get certain kinds of cancers and infections:*
Los Angeles County Animal Care & Control. http://animalcare.lacounty.gov/spay-and-neuter/. Retrieved August 10, 2018.

146 *In 1970, it is estimated that twenty million animals:*
Various sources, e.g., July/August 2008. "Gains in most regions against cat and dog surplus, but no sudden miracles." *Animal People;* Serpell 2017 (citing ASPCA 2014); ASPCA. https://www.aspca.org/animal-homelessness/shelter-intake-and-surrender/pet-statistics. Retrieved May 8, 2017; S. Zawistowski, personal communication, July 18, 2017.

147 *other changes in how we own dogs have also affected euthanization rates:*
Rowan and Kartal 2018.

147 *80 percent of US dogs sterilized:*
Humane Society of the United States, via D. Quenqua. December 2, 2013. "New strides in spaying and neutering." *New York Times.*

147 *Switzerland's Animal Protection Act:*

Swiss Federal Food Safety and Veterinary Office. "Dignity of the animal." https://www.blv.admin.ch/blv/en/home/tiere/tierschutz/wuerde-des-tieres.html. Retrieved August 10, 2018.

148 *spayed and neutered dogs are more likely to gain weight:*

Oberbauer, A. 2017. International Society for Anthrozoology conference, Effective options regarding spay or neuter of dogs, Davis, California; Belanger, J. M., T. P. Bellumori, D. L. Bannasch, et al. 2017. Correlation of neuter status and expression of heritable disorders. *Canine Genetics and Epidemiology*, 4, 6; Lund, E. M., P. J. Armstrong, C. A. Kirk, and J. S. Klausner. 2006. Prevalence and risk factors for obesity in adult dogs from private US veterinary practices. *International Journal of Applied Veterinary Medicine*, 4, 3–5.

148 *trouble with bones and joints:*

See also Karen Becker, in Kerasote, T. 2013. Pukka's Promise: The Quest for Longer-Lived Dogs.

148 *rates of diseases after spaying or neutering:*

Hart, B. 2017. International Society for Anthrozoology conference. Effective options regarding spay or neuter of dogs. Davis, California.

148 *changes in behavior after spaying or neutering:*

Hart 2017.

152 *one percent chance of death under anesthesia:*

Accounts of the risks of death during anesthesia vary greatly. But this 1 percent figure is borne out in a number of studies, e.g., Bille, C., V. Auvigne, S. Libermann, et al. 2012. Risk of anaesthetic mortality in dogs and cats: An observational cohort study of 3546 cases. *Veterinary Anaesthesia and Analgesia*, 39, 59–68.

Chapter 14: HUMORLESS

158 *It's humiliating to pretend that dogs are something that they are not:*

Gruen, L. 2014. Dignity, captivity, and an ethics of sight. In L. Gruen, ed. *The Ethics of Captivity*, ch. 14.

160 *living a full life as a dog:*

Nussbaum, M. C. 2004. Beyond "compassion and humanity": Justice for nonhuman animals. In Sunstein and Nussbaum, eds., pp. 299–320.

Chapter 15: TAIL OF THE DOG

164 *the words we use about dogs:*

"Hangdog" comes from Barnette, M. 2003. *Dog Days and Dandelions: A Lively Guide to the Animal Meanings behind Everyday Words*. For more on doggy words see Serpell 2017; see also Pfister, D. S. 2017. Against the droid's "instrument of efficiency," for animalizing technologies in a posthumanist spirit. *Philosophy & Rhetoric*, 50, 201–227.

ACKNOWLEDGMENTS

Thanks, specifically, to the following people for their thoughts, knowledge, and their time on one or more matter of dogly relevance:

"The Perfect Name": Stanley Brandes, Bob Fagen, Jesse Scheidlower, Richard Zacks

"Owning Dogs": David Favre, Stephen Zawistowski

"Things People Say to Their Dogs": Keith Olbermann and all owners who completed the questionnaire

"The Trouble with Breeds": Bronwen Dickey, Brynn White—librarian extraordinaire at the AKC Library, Stephen Zawistowski, the veterinarians and staff at the University of Florida College of Veterinary Medicine's Maddie's Shelter Medicine Program

"Dog Stuff": Katherine Grier (and her well-thumbed book), Daniel Hurewitz, Brynn White

"The Dog in the Mirror": Dan Charnas (you dawg)

"Against Sex": Amy Attas, Thierry Bedossa, Cynda Crawford and others at Maddie's Shelter Medicine Program, Anne-Lil Kvam, Cindy Otto, Stephen Zawistowski

"Humorless": Honor Jones at the *New York Times*, Kirsten Van Vlandren at the Colonial Theater

"Tail of the Dog": Ammon Shea

Thank you, more generally, to nearly a decade of students in Canine Cognition, and over a decade of researchers at the Horowitz Dog Cognition Lab, for continuing conversations about dogs; to the ever-willing owners and cooperative and charming dogs who participate in our studies; and to April Benson, for her generous support of the Lab.

The New York Society Library, Barnard College, and Roe Jan Library provided quiet places to work and productive air to breathe, for which I am thankful.

Thanks to Becca Franks and Jeff Sebo, who have stimulated my thinking about a number of issues in this book; to Wendy Walters, for her essays; to Valeria Luiselli and Jesús Rodriguez-Velasco, for ideas about medieval manuscripts that inspired my thinking about marginalia; to Julie Tate for her thorough fact-checking of "Against Sex," "The Trouble with Breeds," and "Owning Dogs"; and to Elizabeth and Jay, who instilled in me a love of animals, a love of thinking clearly, and a love of questioning the perceived wisdom. For their friendship and conversations about books, thanks to Meakin Armstrong, Betsy Carter, Catherine Chung, Alison Curry, Daniel Hurewitz, Elizabeth Kadetsky, Maira Kalman, Sally Koslow, Aryn Kyle, Susan Orlean, Aaron Retica, Timea Szell, Jennifer Vanderbes, and Bill Vourvoulias.

I owe everyone at Scribner great thanks for continuing to follow me follow my dogs: especially Susan Moldow, Nan Graham, and Roz Lippel. And especially-especially,

I am privileged and grateful to continue to have Colin Harrison as reader and editor, and Sarah Goldberg as critical art eye. Jaya Miceli, Kara Watson, Ashley Gilliam, Brian Belfiglio, Abigail Novak, thanks for helping this book come to life—and thanks to Christian Purdy for helping it fly.

If there's got to be a camera pointing at me, I'm always glad that Vegar Abelsnes is behind it. I appreciate his constancy: his photos of me with Finnegan are a record of our life together: beginning in 2008, with *Inside of a Dog* (Finn: age 1), continuing through 2012, 2015, and now, 2019 (Finn: age 11)—even if it is Edsel who made the jacket.

Thanks to Kris Dahl at ICM for many freewheeling, brainstorming conversations, and her steadfast advocacy.

Thanks to Ammon and Ogden, for looking at, walking with, and talking about dogs with me. And again to Ammon, for the generosity of his enthusiasm about each new topic. To Damon, for thinking out loud with me. And again to Ogden, for lending me the drawing on this page.

You can't know how much I thank you, Finnegan and Upton—and the countless other dogs who have met my gaze. I'm so glad to know you all.

INDEX

Instructions dog talker category, 58–60, 62